I0484882

# George Luks:
# 99 Colour Plates

**By Maria Tsaneva**

**First Edition**

\*\*\*\*\*

## George Luks: 99 Colour Plates
\*\*\*\*\*

# Foreword

*"I can paint with a shoestring dipped in pitch and lard . . . Technique did you say? My slats! . . . It's in you or it isn't. Who taught Shakespeare technique? Guts! Life! Life! That's my technique."* - George Benjamin Luks

George Benjamin Luks (1867 – 1933) was an American realist artist and illustrator. His vigorously painted genre paintings of urban subjects are examples of the Ashcan School of American art. He studied at the Pennsylvania Academy of Fine Art under Thomas Anshutz and traveled abroad studying from 1885-1895. Luks first met the group of artists known as "The Eight" while working as a newspaper artist in Philadelphia in the 1890s. Luks subject matter generally focused on the everyday immediacy and drama of the working class people. He was able to portray their energy and raw physicality.

In the 1920s, he shifted to the harshness of coalmining. "The wrestlers" (1905) is perhaps one of Luks most widely reproduced works which shows his ability to capture the essence of the moment with clarity mixed with a reckless approach to technique and anatomy. Luks was one of the founders of the AAPS, which organized the 1913 Armory Show as well as being an influential teacher at the Art Students League

Luks was a born rebel and one of the most distinctive personalities in American art. "He is Puck. He is Caliban. He is Falstaff," his contemporary, the art critic James Gibbons Huneker, wrote. He took pride in being known as the "bad boy" of American art, liked to characterize himself as entirely self-created, and downplayed the influence of Robert Henri, or any contemporary, on his artistic development.

He was equally at home at a prize fight or in a tavern as in a museum or a gallery. Luks was always a heavy drinker. Although many sources confirm this tendency, they also characterize him as a man with a kind heart who befriended people living on the edge who became subjects for his works of art. Luks created portraits of the urban poor, explaining that he liked the slums because "down there people are what they are." Examples of this are numerous: e.g., Widow McGee (1902) or The Old Duchess and The Rag Picker in which Luks depicted with sensitivity elderly, down-and-out women who knew the harsh realities of the street.

Luks was a paradox: a man of enormous egotism and a great generosity of spirit. Luks was found dead in a doorway by a policeman in the early morning hours of October 29, 1933 following a bar room brawl. Ira Glackens, the son of William Glackens, wrote about Luks's death that, contrary to the newspaper account stating that the painter had succumbed on his way to paint the dawn sky, he had been beaten to death in an altercation with one of the other customers at a nearby bar.

His packed funeral was attended by family, former students, and past and present friends. Luks was married twice but had no children. He is buried at Fernwood Cemetery in Royersford, Pennsylvania.

# Paintings

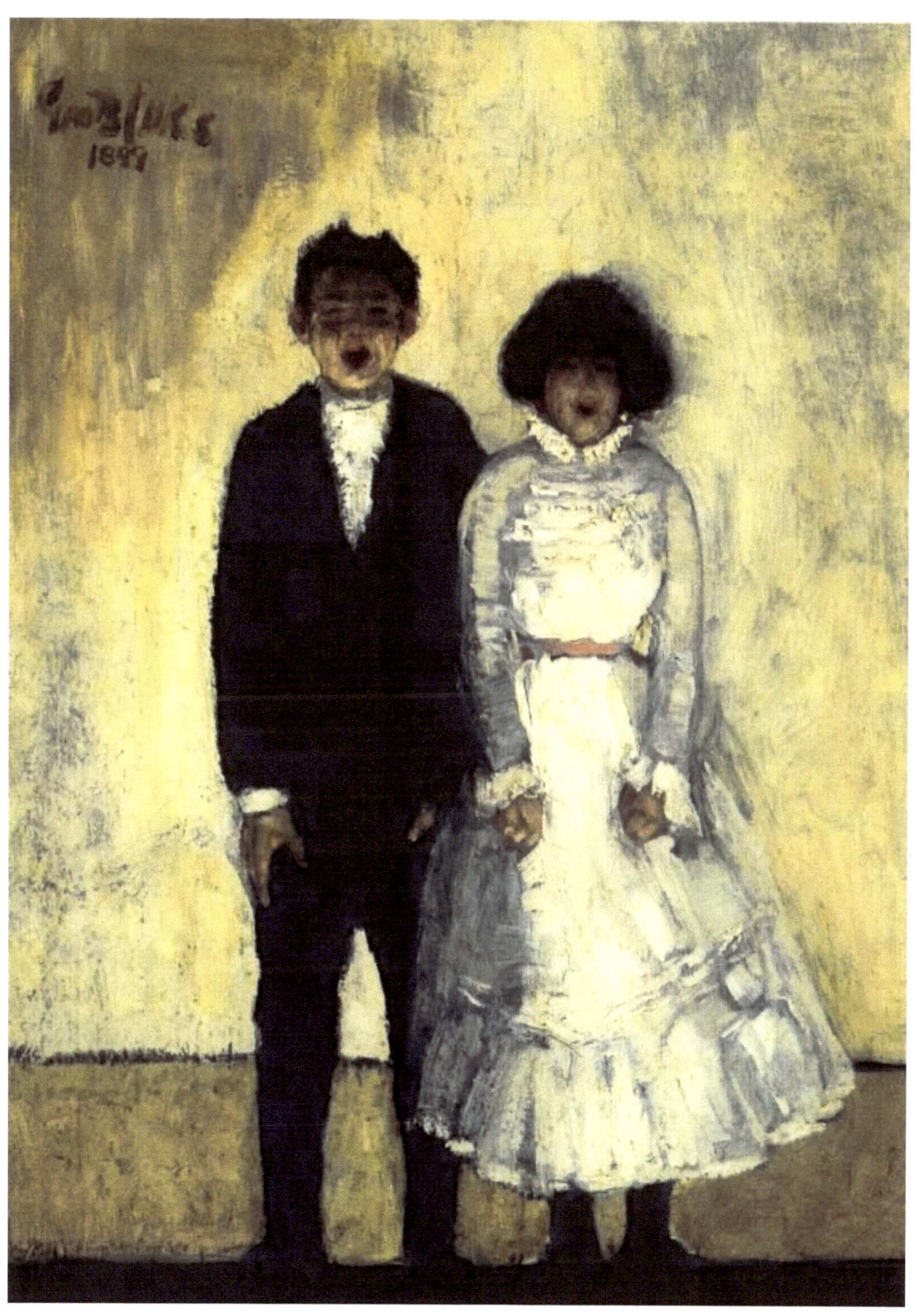

The Amateurs 1899
Oil on canvas

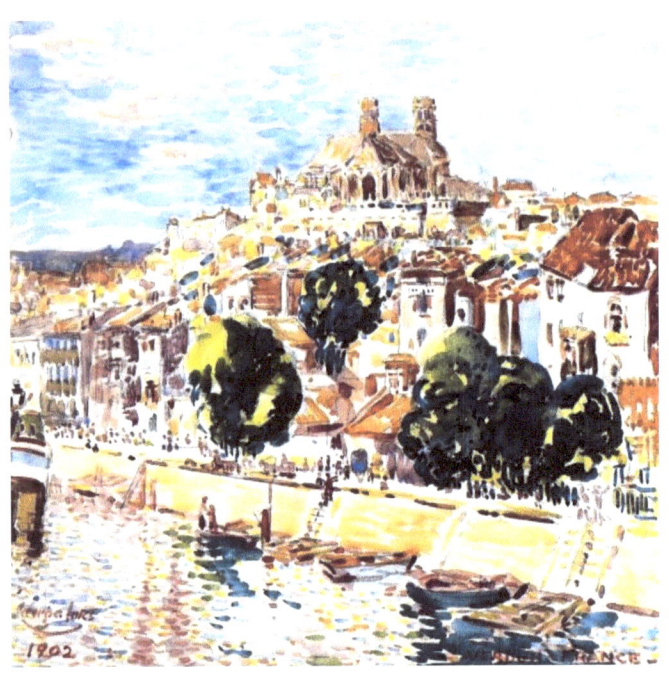

Verdun, France, 1902
Oil on canvas

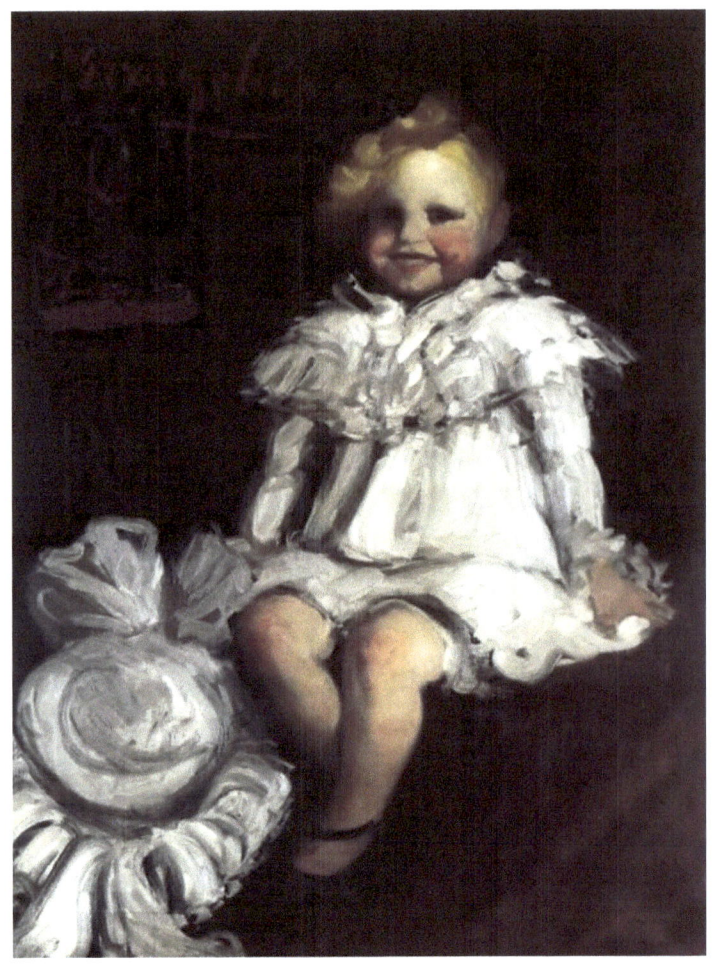

Little Lore with Her Hat, 1904
Oil on canvas

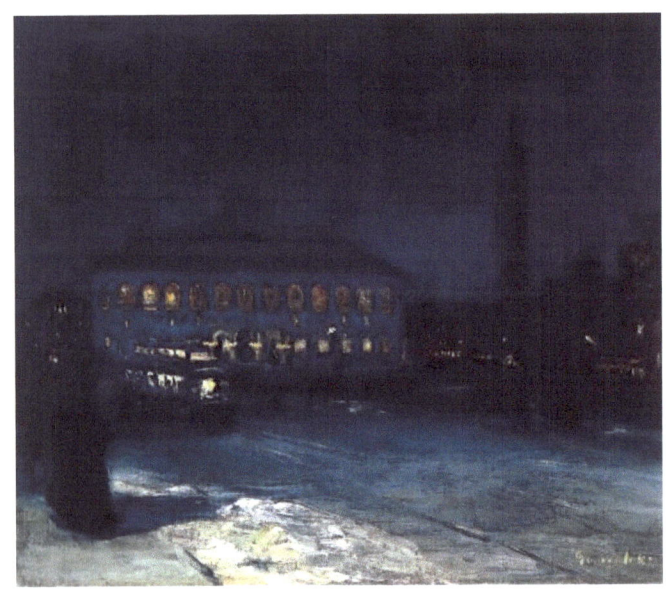

Copley Square, 1904
Oil on canvas

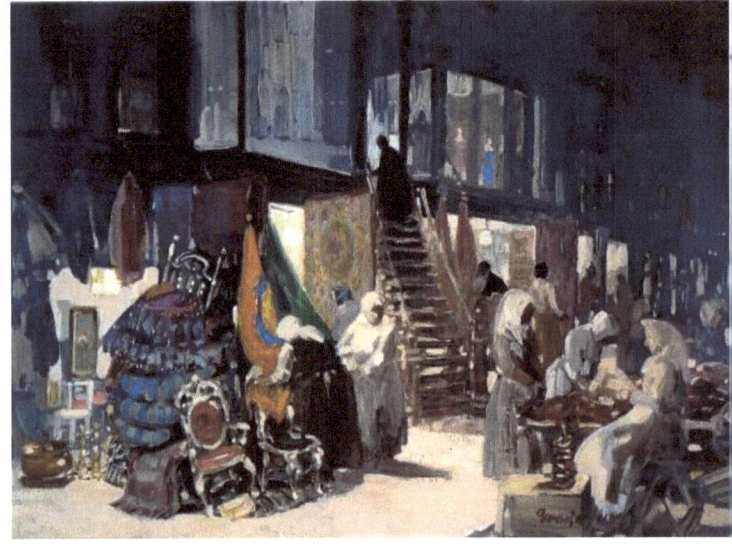

Allen Street, 1905
Oil on canvas

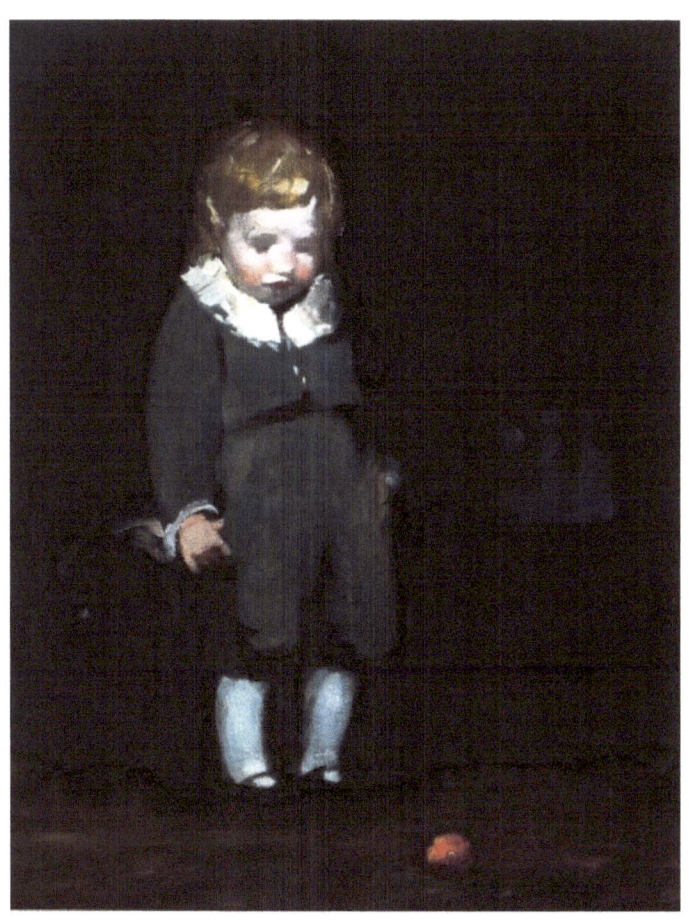

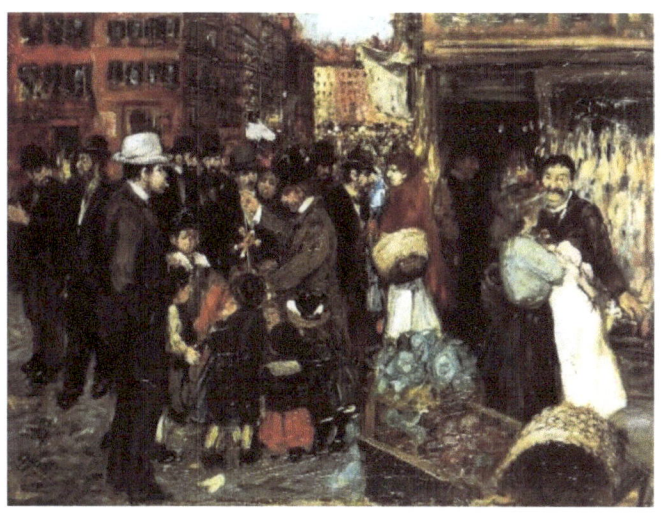

Hester Street 1905, Oil on canvas

Child in Grey, 1905
Oil on canvas

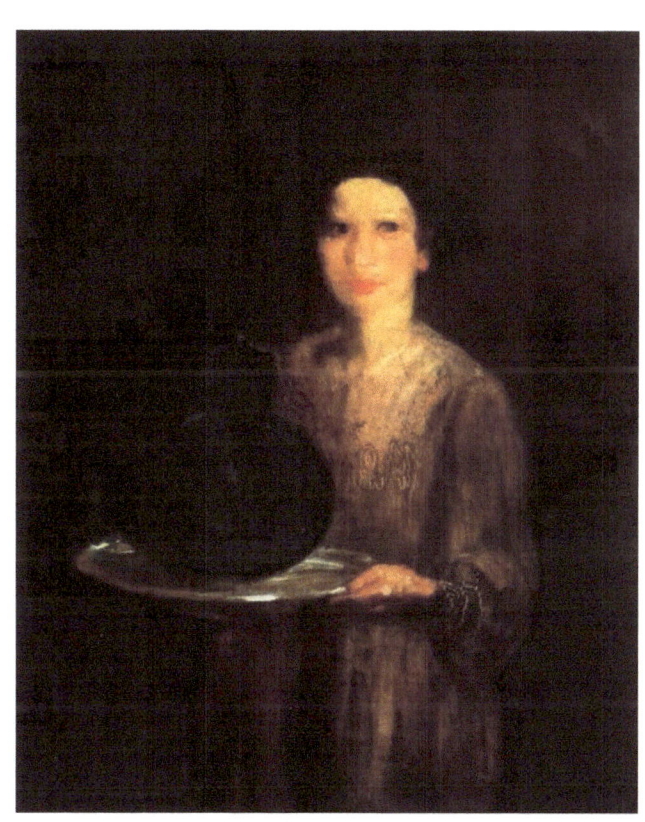

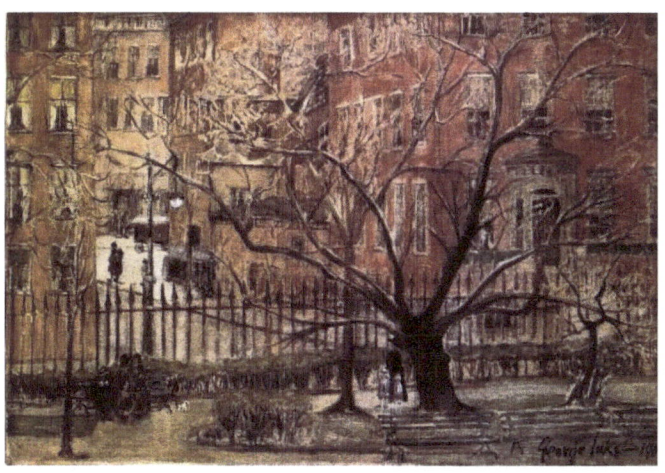

The Pawnbroker's Daughter, 1905
Oil on canvas

Gramercy Park 1905, Oil on canvas

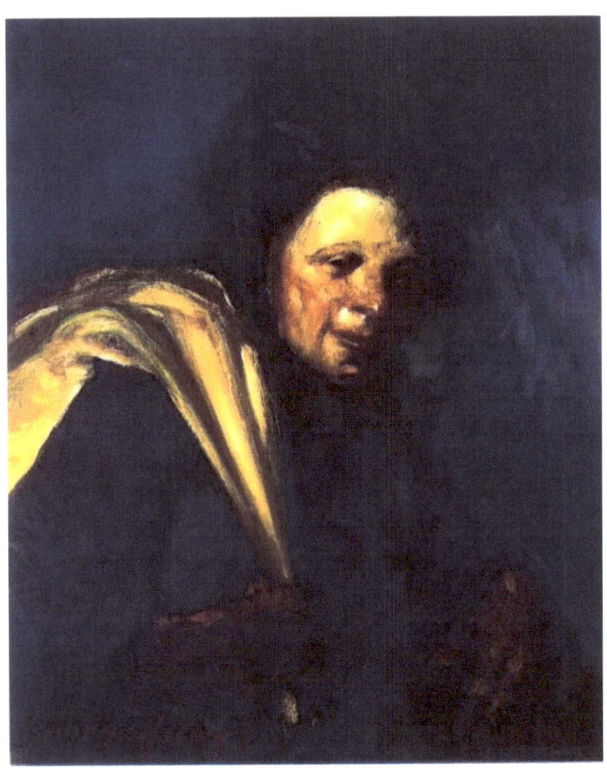

The Rag Picker, 1905
Oil on canvas

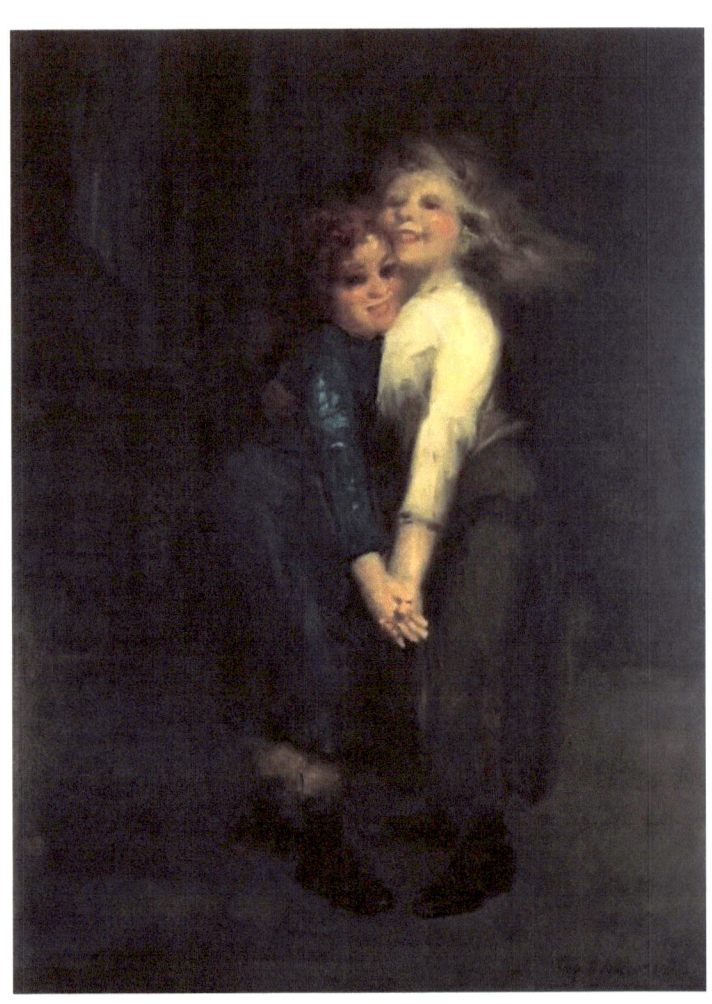

The Spielers, 1905
Oil on canvas

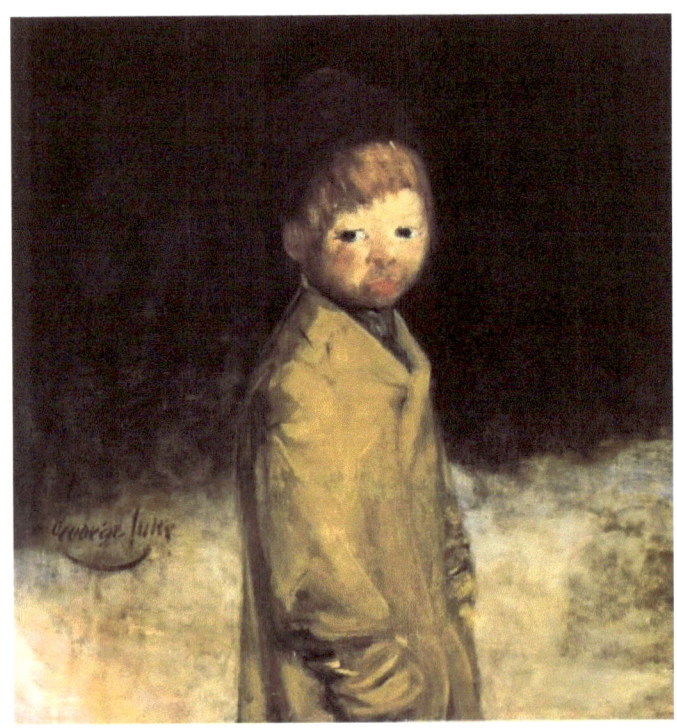

The Sand Artist
Oil on canvas

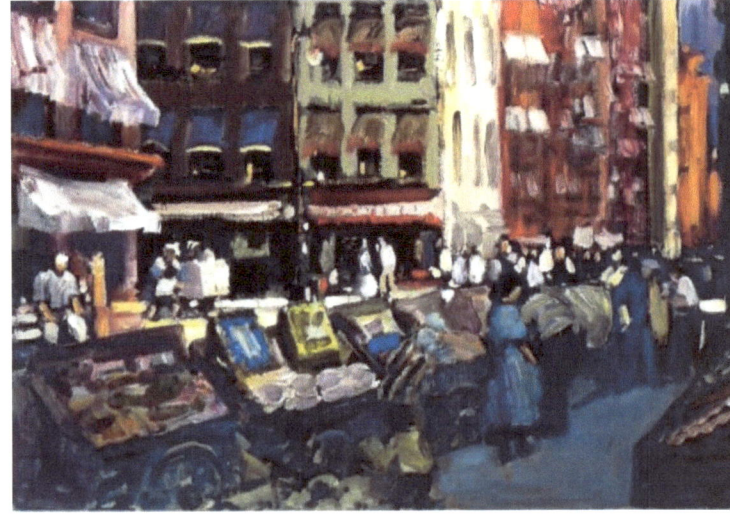

Thompson and Bleecker Streets, 1905
Oil on canvas

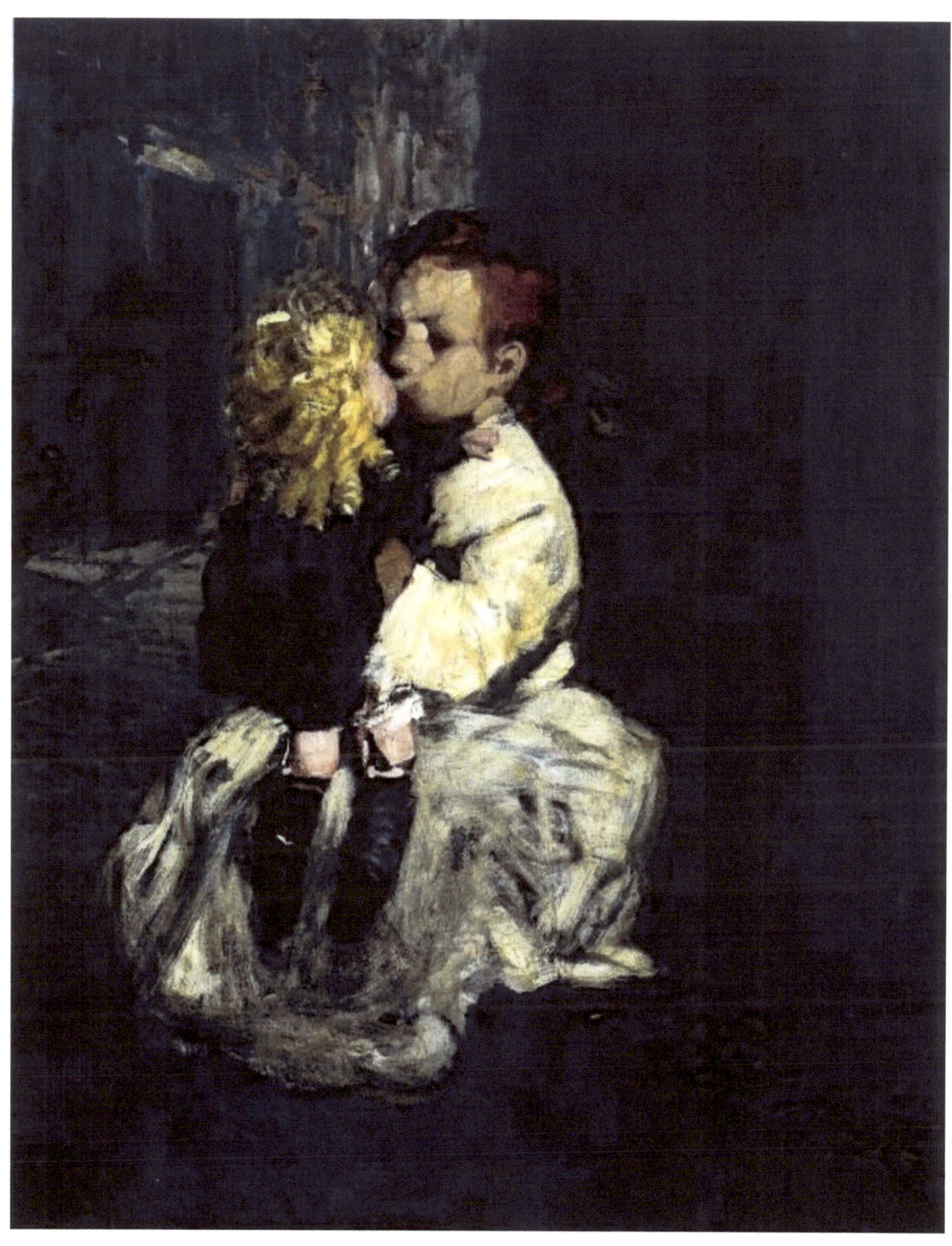

The Little Madonna, 1907
Oil on canvas

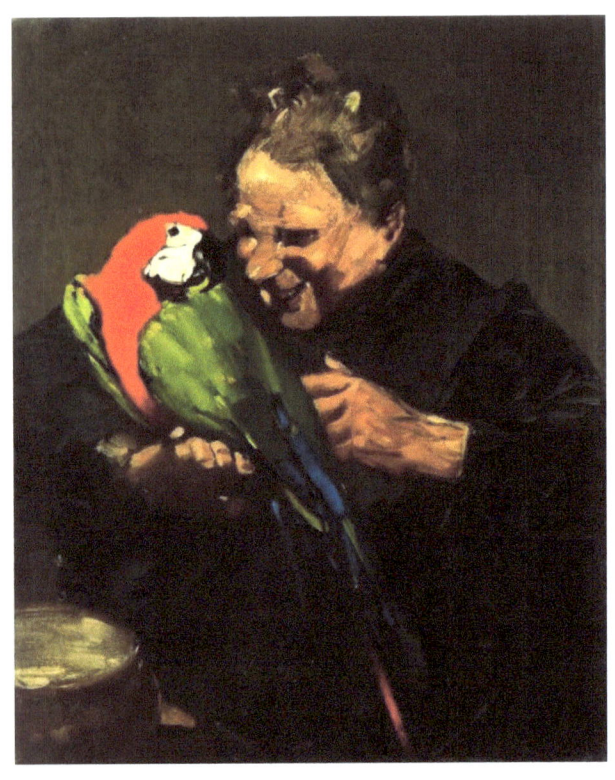

Pals, 1907
Oil on canvas

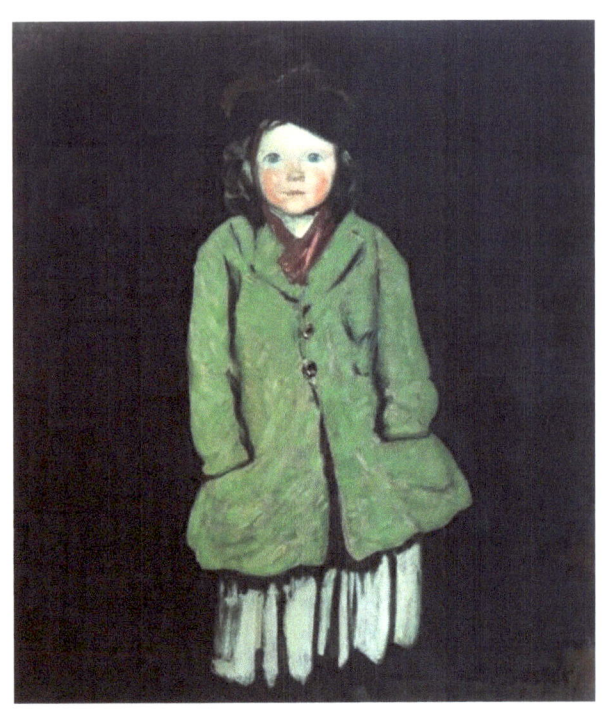

Lily Williams, 1909
Oil on canvas

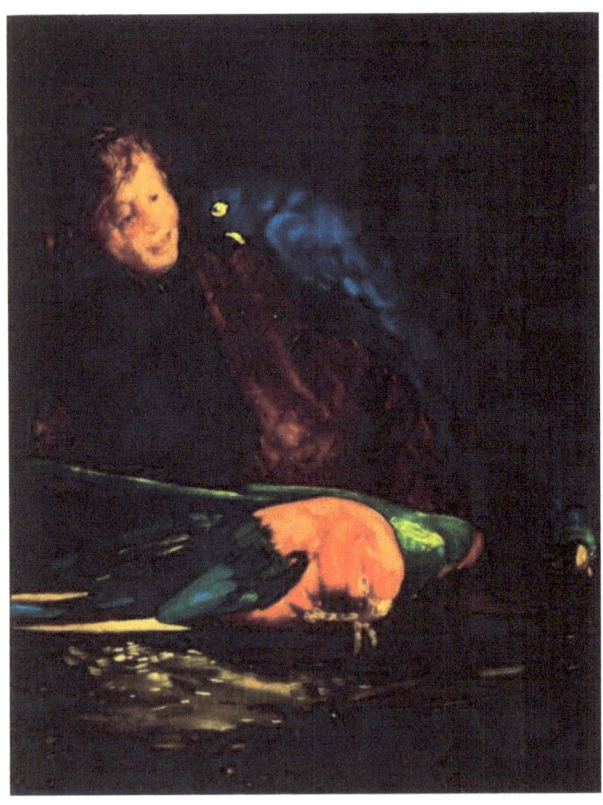

Woman and Macaws, 1907
Oil on canvas

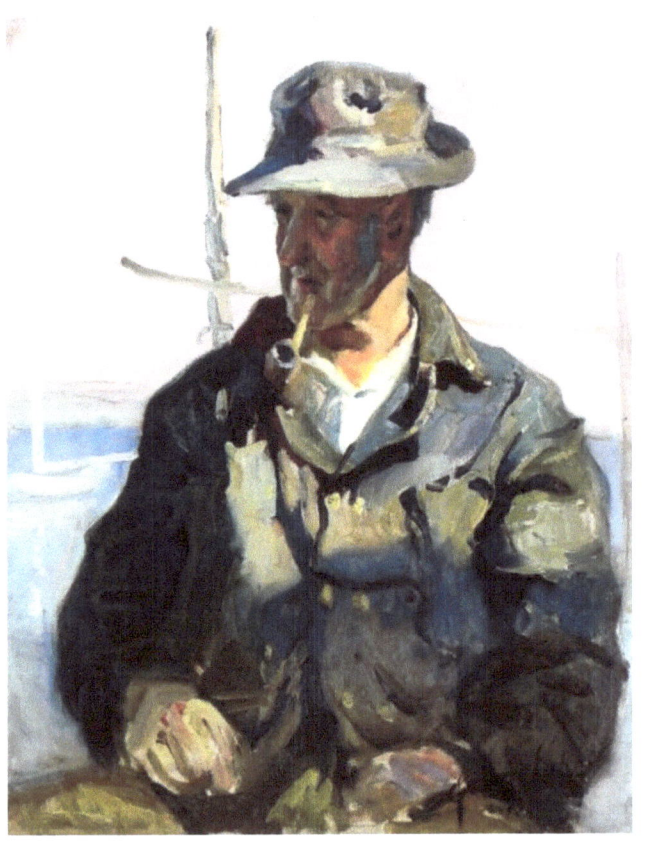

Old Salt, 1909
Oil on canvas

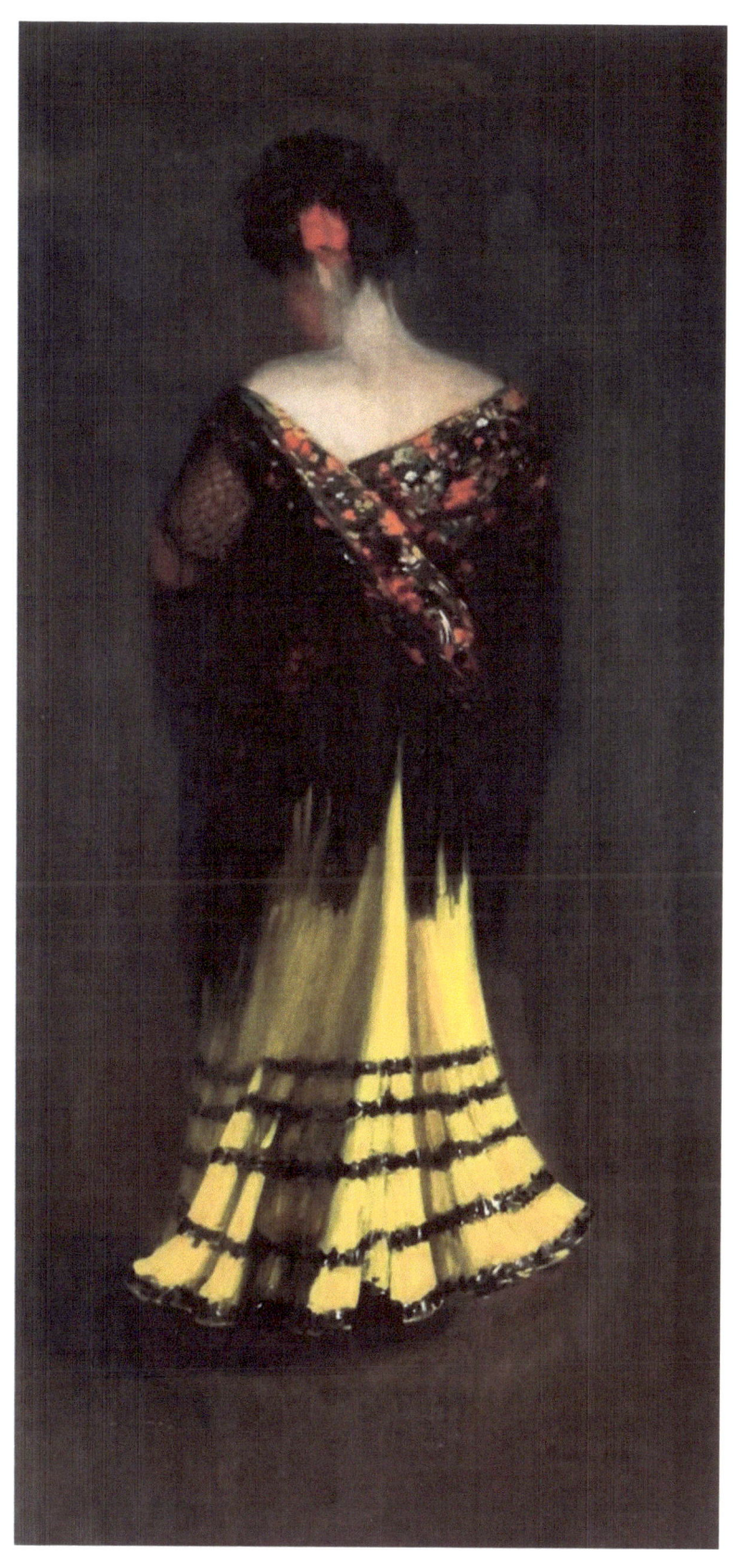

The Spanish Shawl: Portrait of Jeanne Frankenberg 1910
Oil on canvas

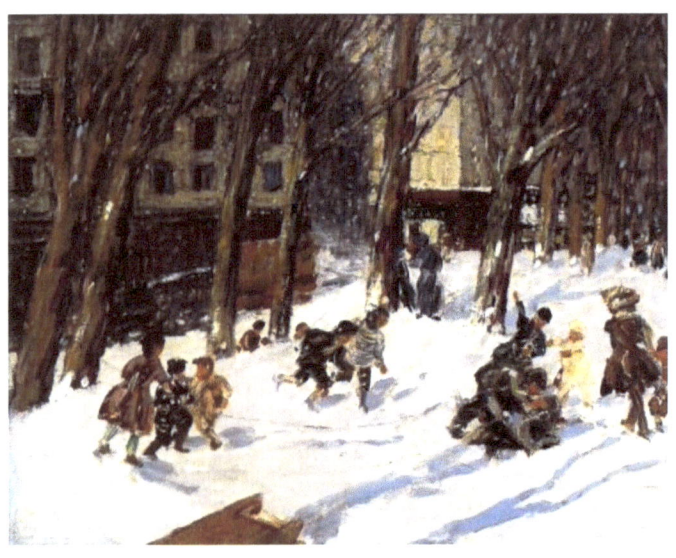

Winter - High Bridge Park 1913, Oil on
canvas

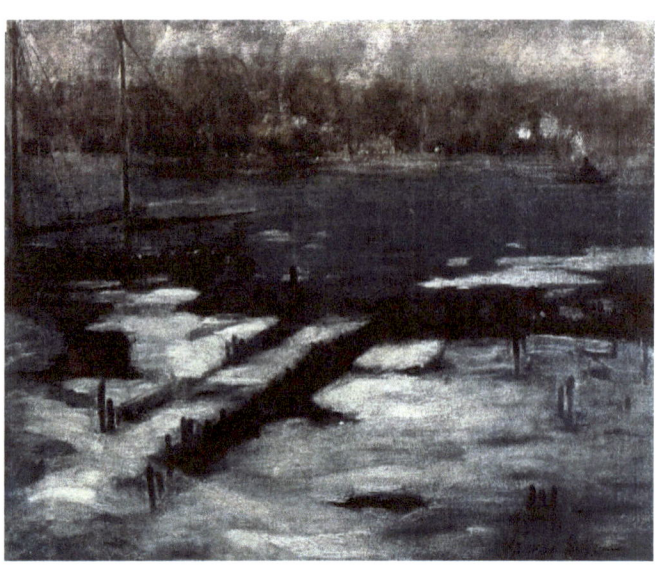

The North River, New York, 1910
Oil on canvas

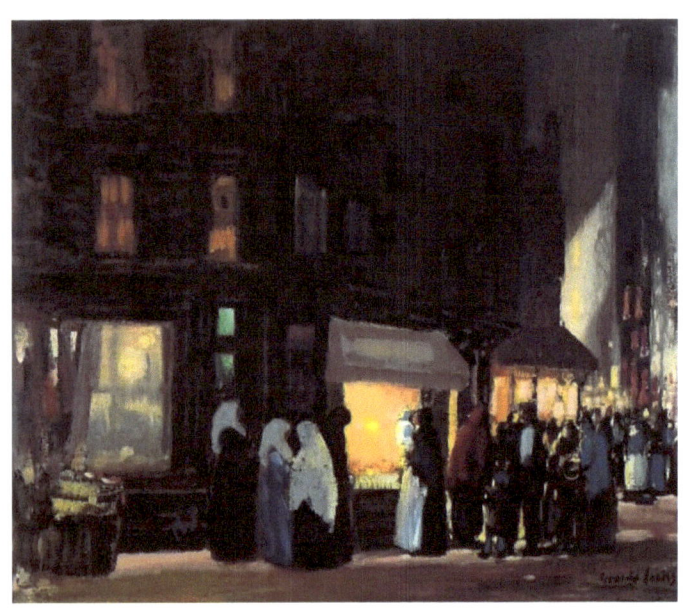

Winter - High Bridge Park 1915, Oil on
canvas

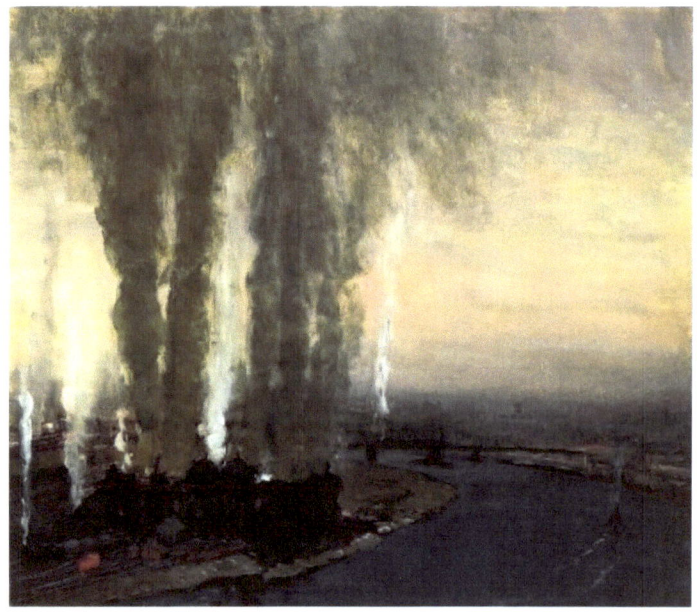

Roundhouse at High Bridge, 1910
Oil on canvas

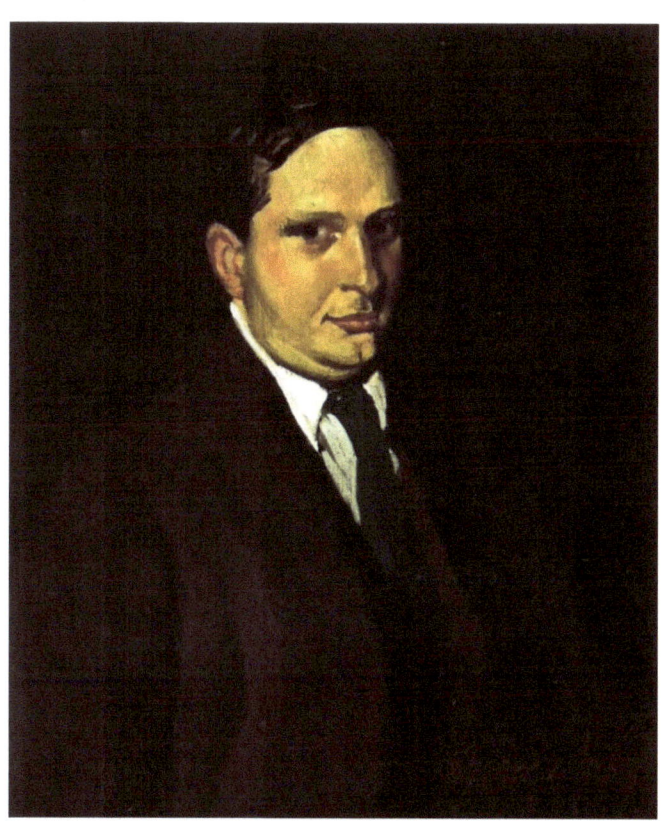

The Green Tie, 1915
Oil on canvas

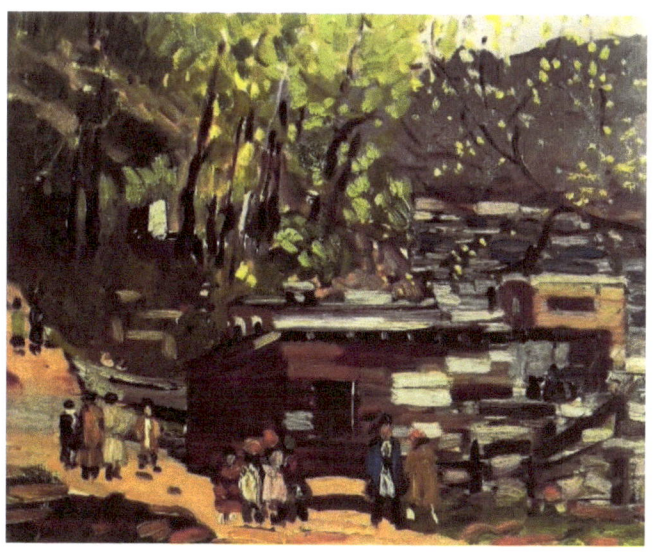

Upper Manhattan, 1915
Oil on canvas

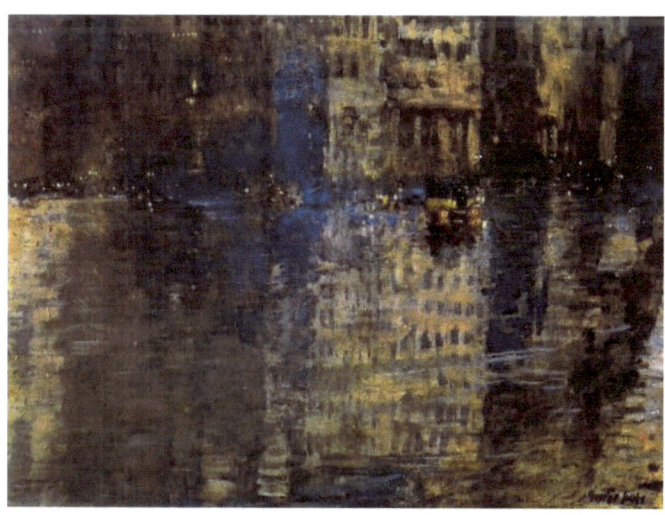

Madison Square, 1915
Oil on canvas

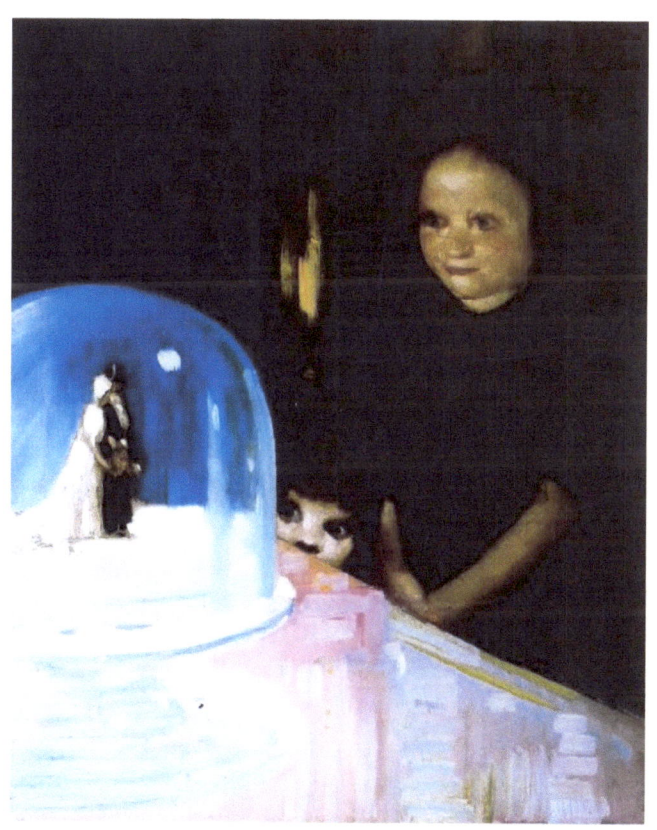

The Wedding Cake, 1915
Oil on canvas

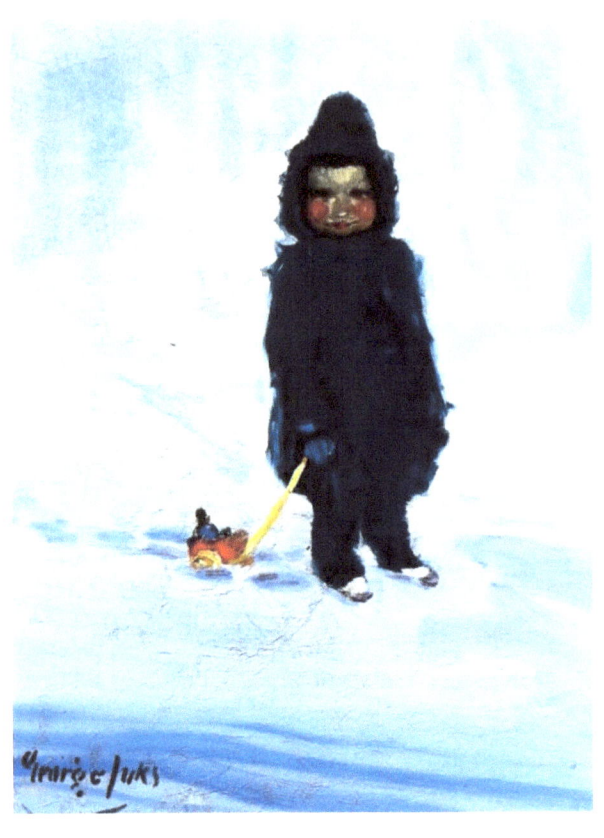

Child with Wagon, 1916
Oil on canvas

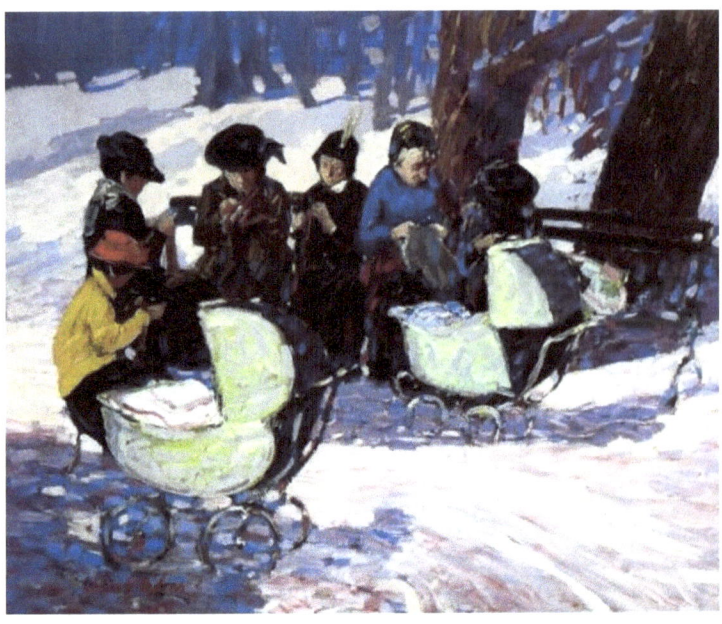

Knitting for the Soldiers: High Bridge Park
1918, Oil on canvas

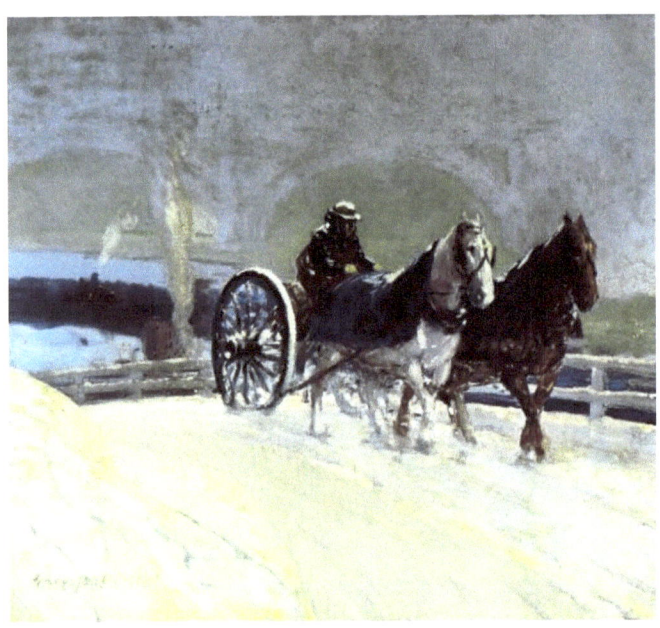

Hitch Team, 1916
Oil on canvas

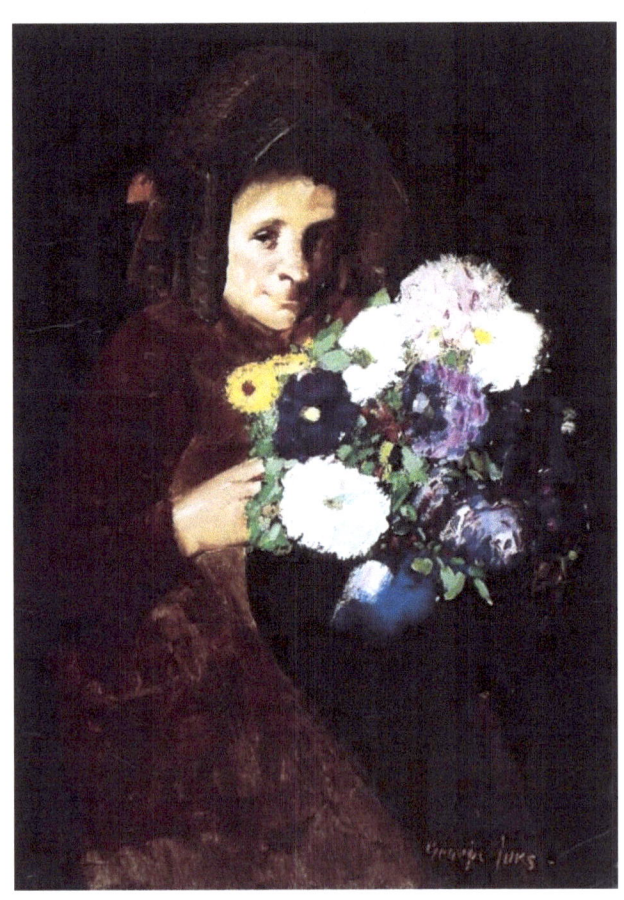

Old Flower Woman, 1918
Oil on canvas

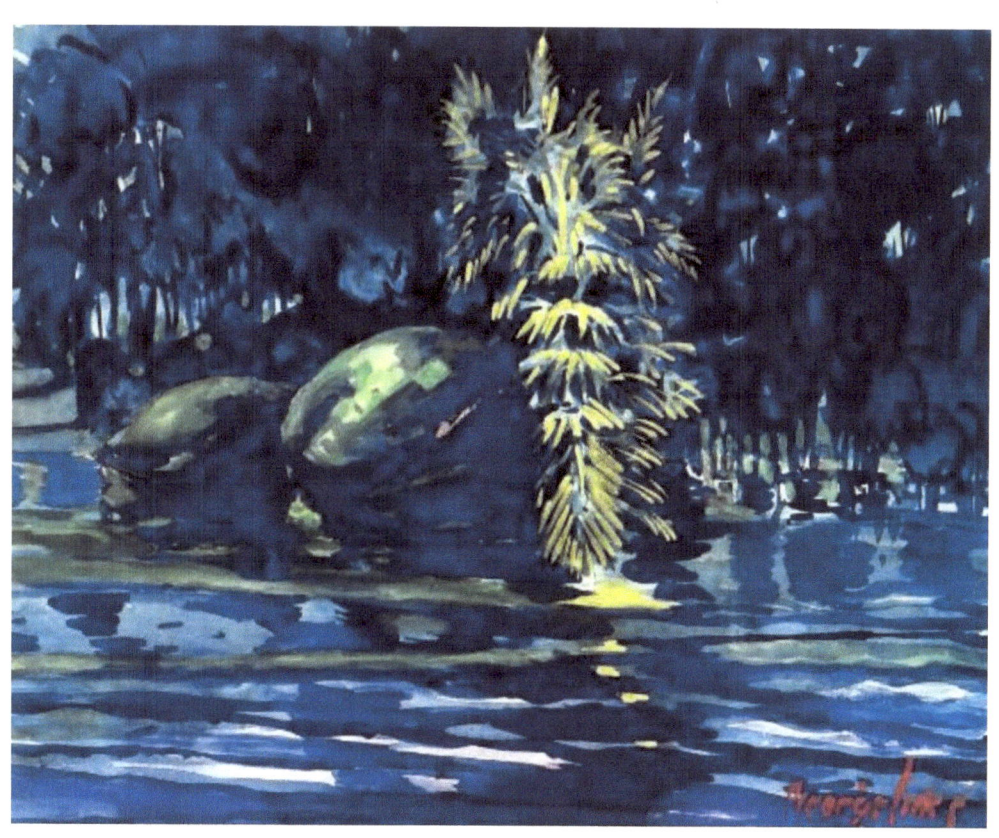

Boulders on a Riverbank, 1918
Oil on canvas

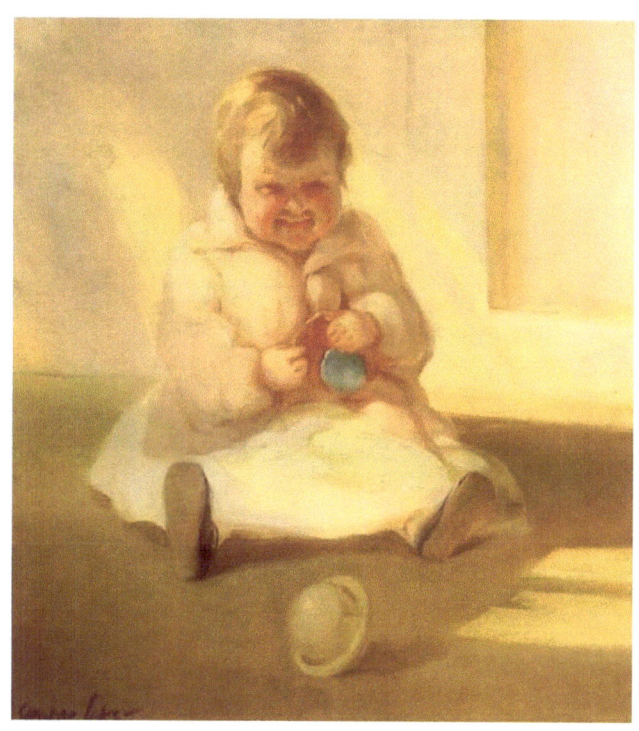

Child with a Toy, 1919
Oil on canvas

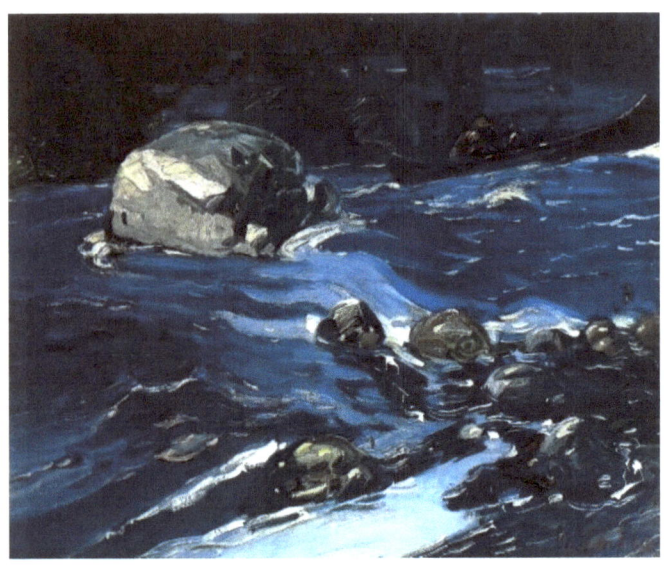

Climbing the Screecher, 1919
Oil on canvas

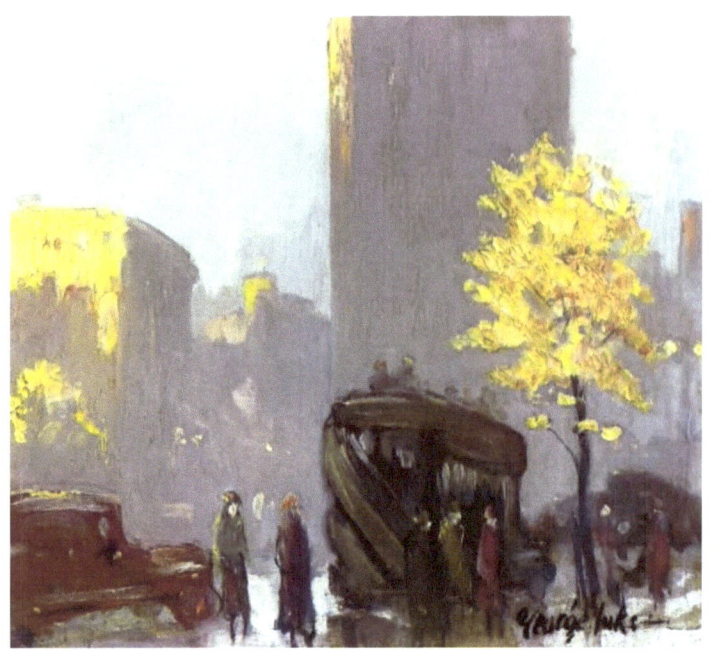

Fifth Avenue, New York, 1920
Oil on canvas

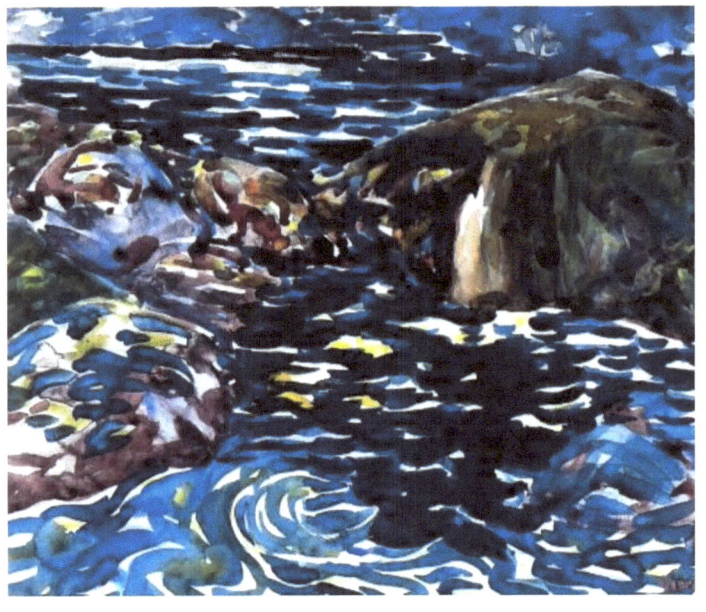

The Eddy, 1919
Oil on canvas

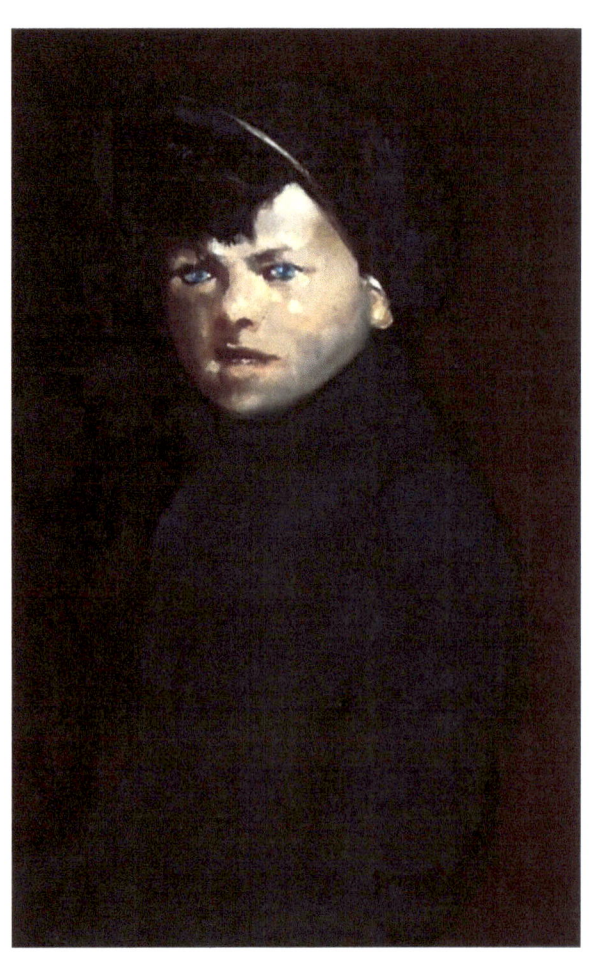

Flyweight Champion of Jumel Place, 1920
Oil on canvas

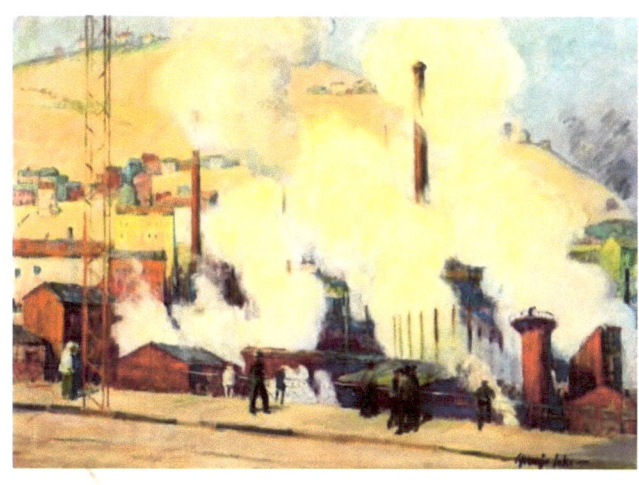

Industrial Scene, Pottsville, Pennsylvania, 1920
Oil on canvas

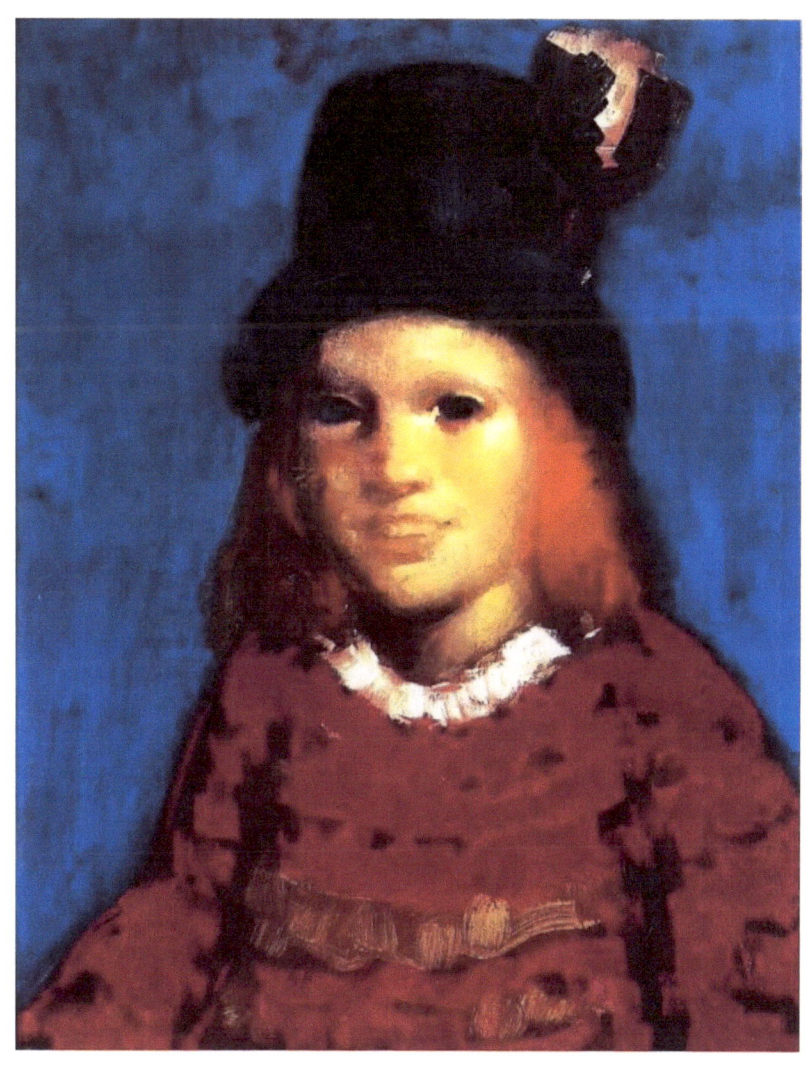

Little Girl in a Top Hat, 1920
Oil on canvas

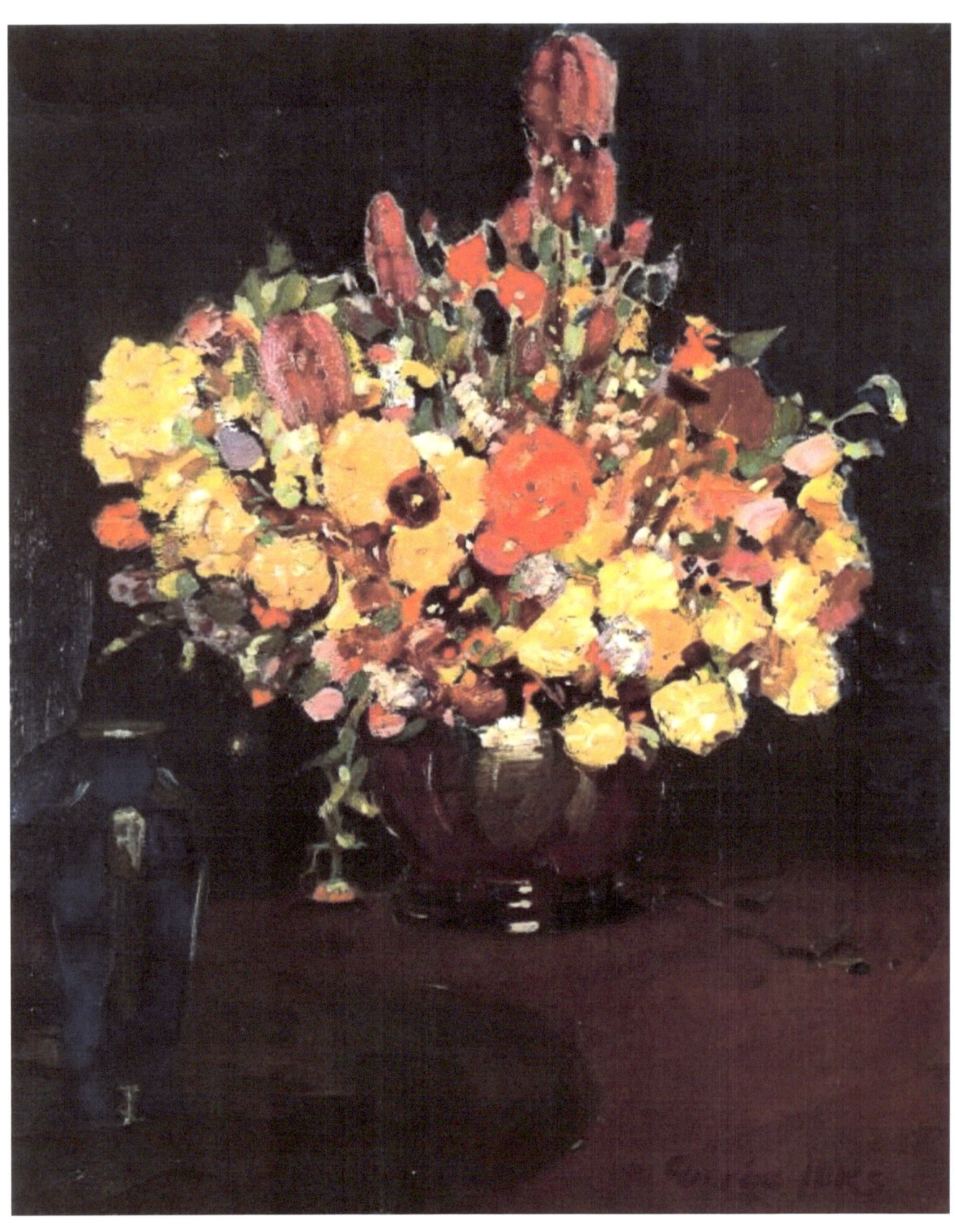

October Flowers 1920
Oil on canvas

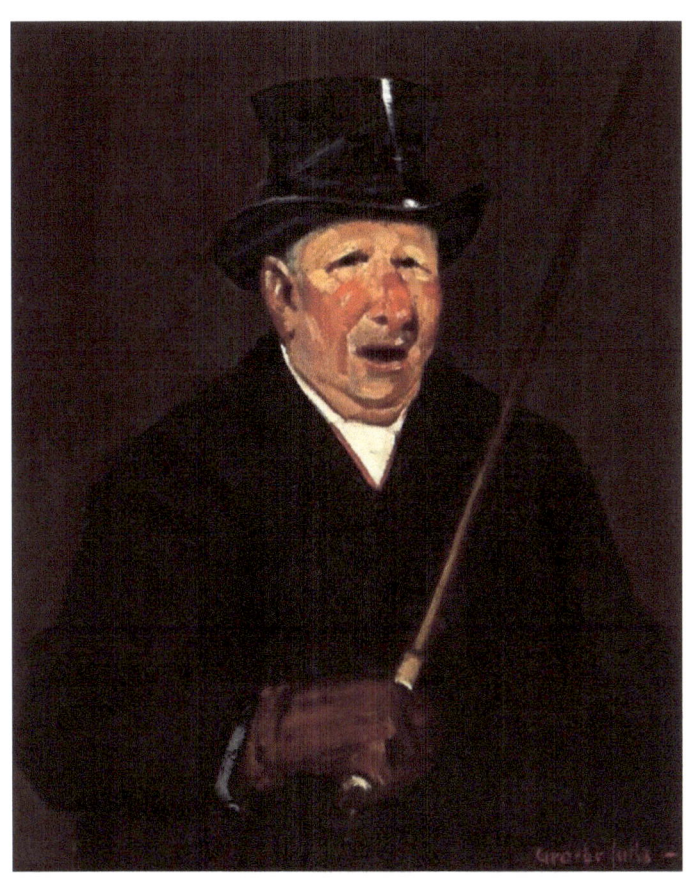

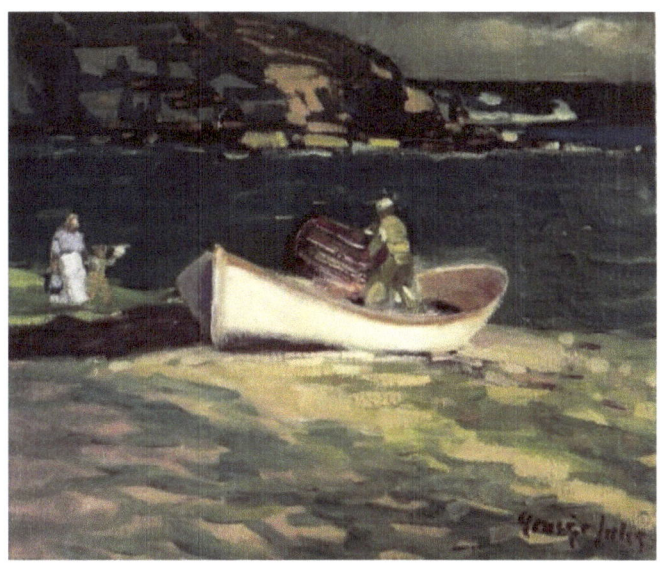

Fisherman, Cape Elizabeth, Maine, 1922
Oil on canvas

The Cabby, 1921
Oil on canvas

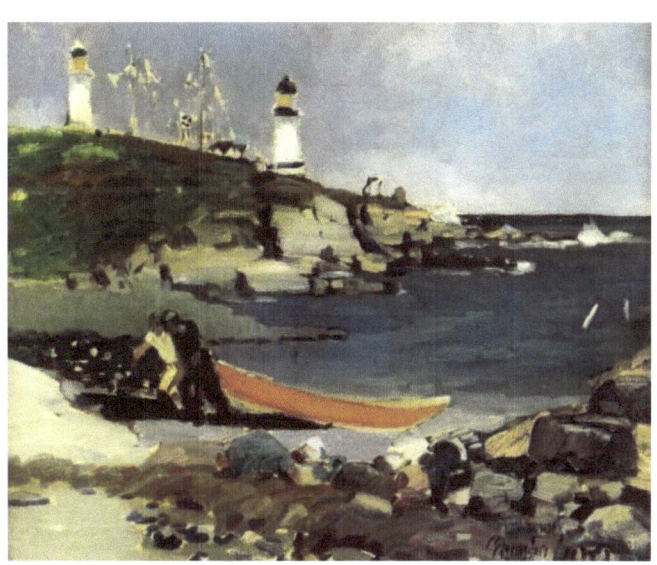

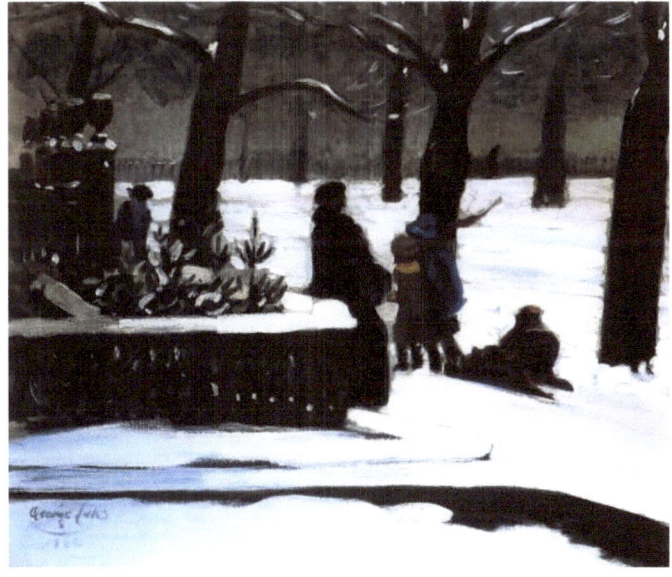

Hannaford's Cove 1922
Oil on canvas

Commonwealth Ave, Boston, 1922
Oil on canvas

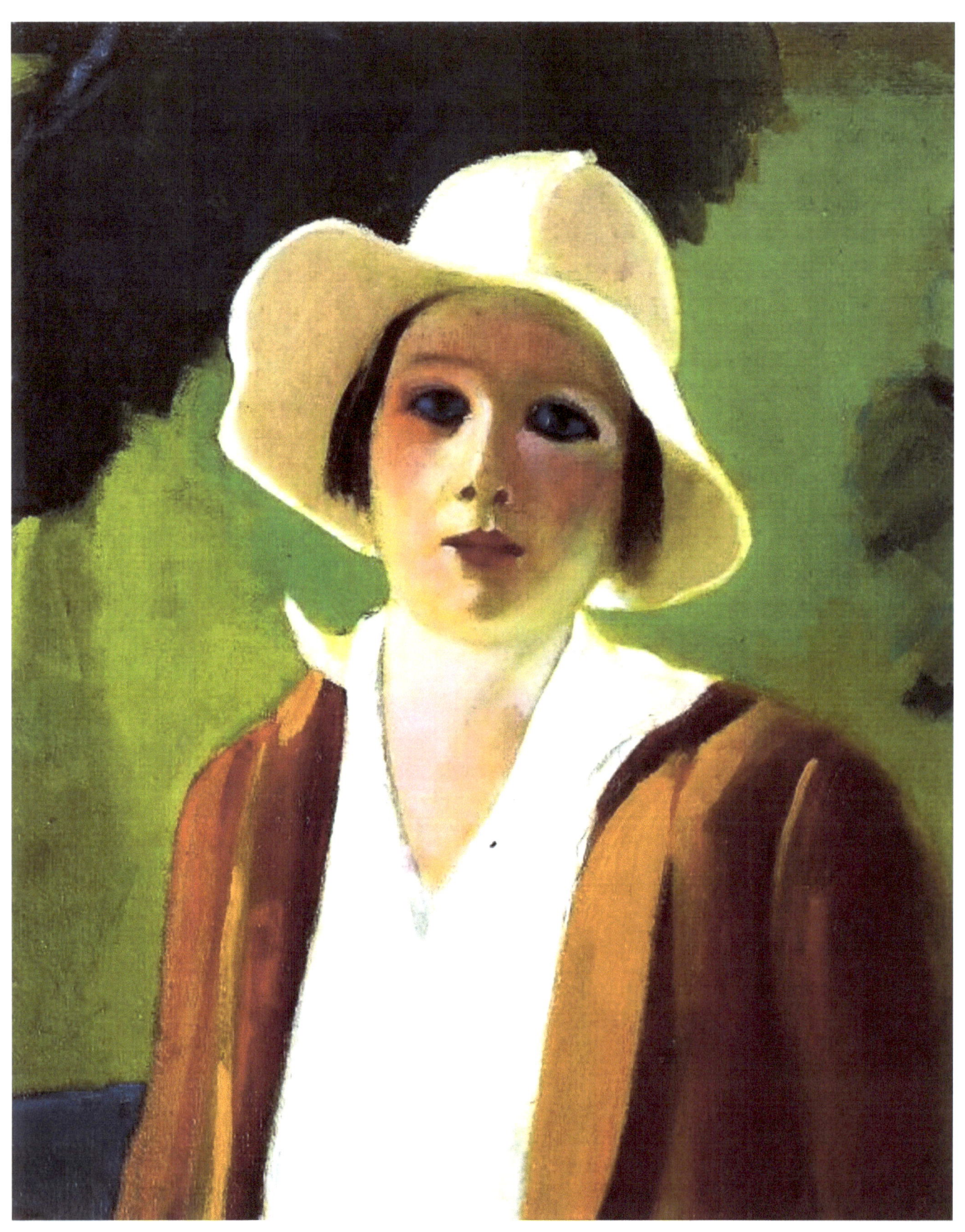

Lady with White Hat, 1922
Oil on canvas

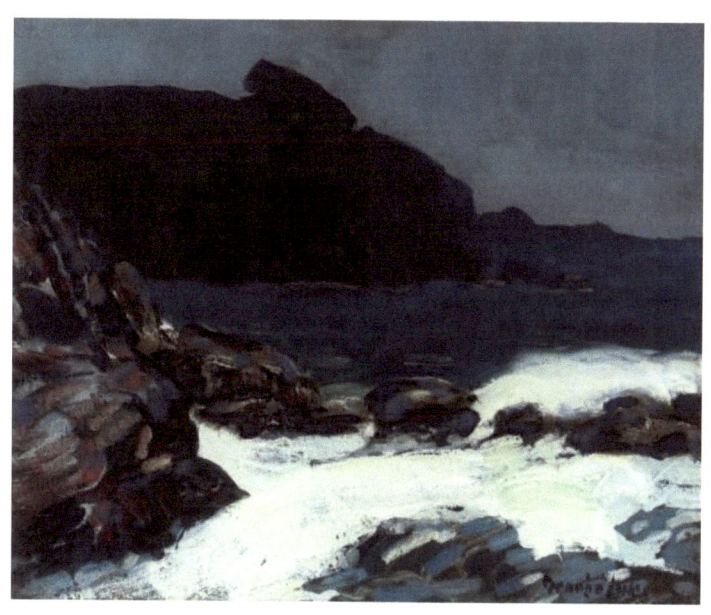

The Ledge, 1922
Oil on canvas

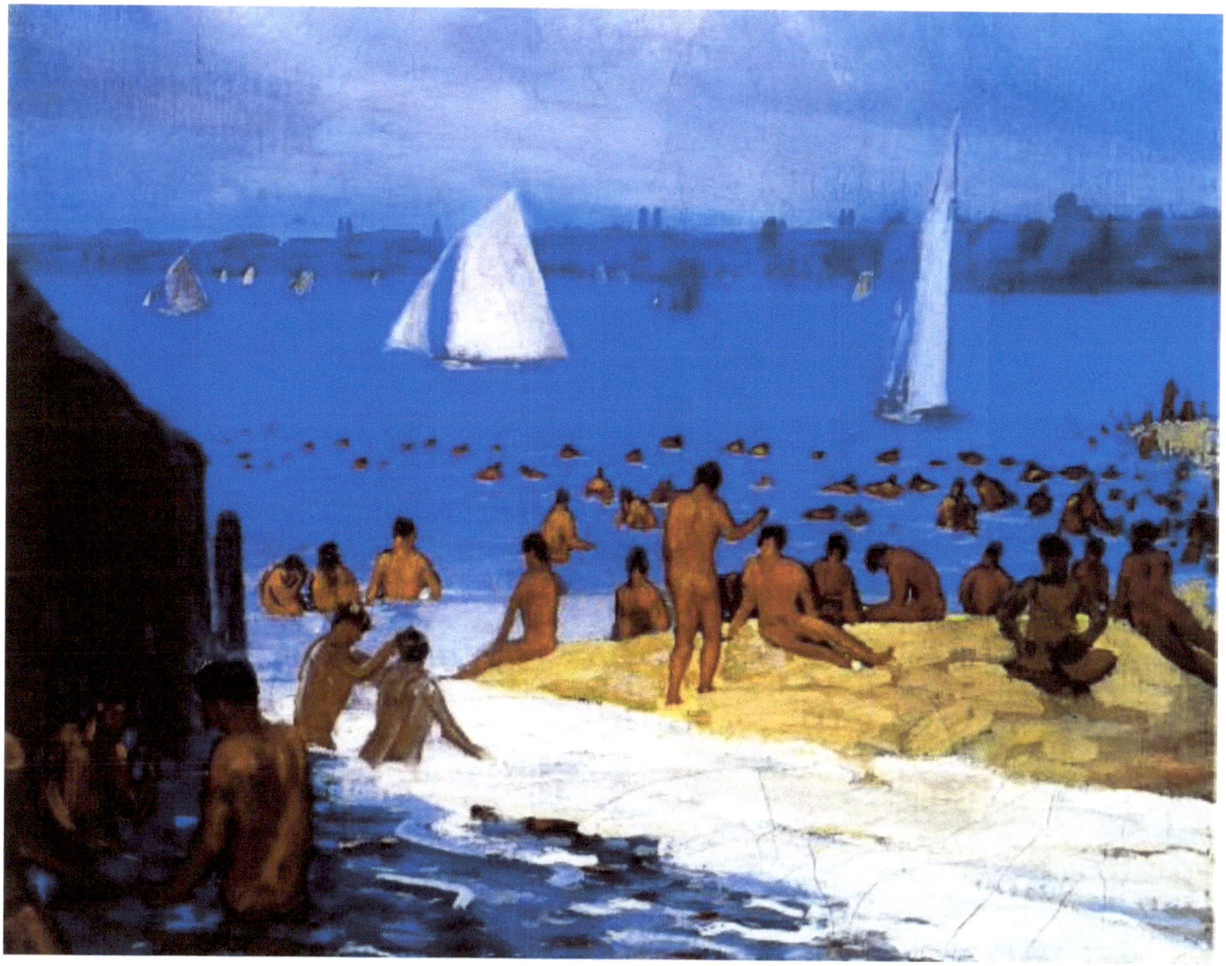

The L Street Brownies, 1922
Oil on canvas

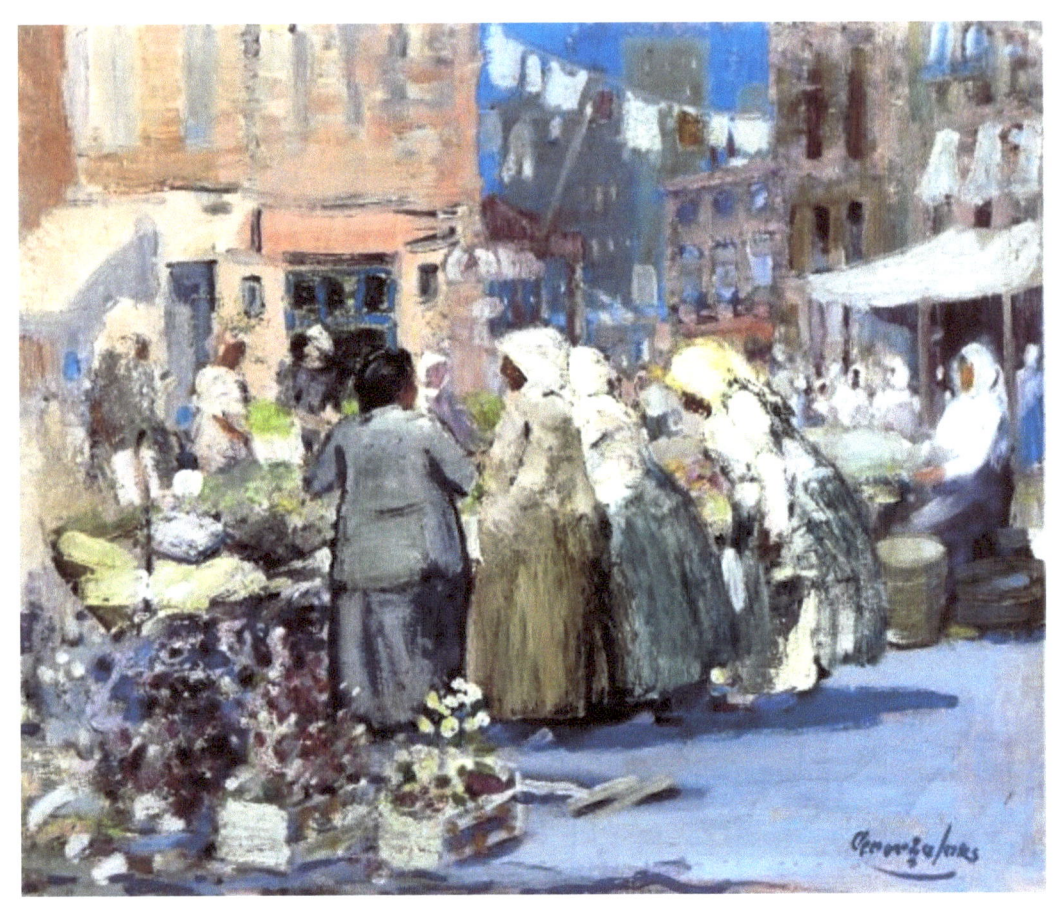

Spring Morning, Houston and Division Streets, New York, 1922
Oil on canvas

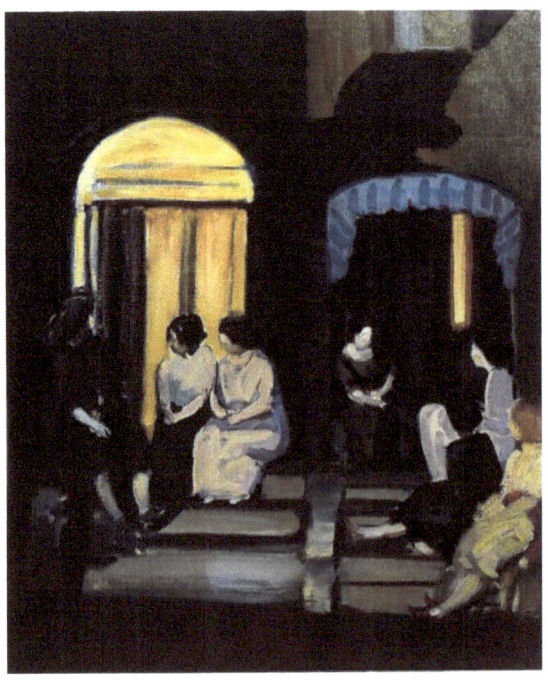

St. Botolph Street, 1922
Oil on canvas

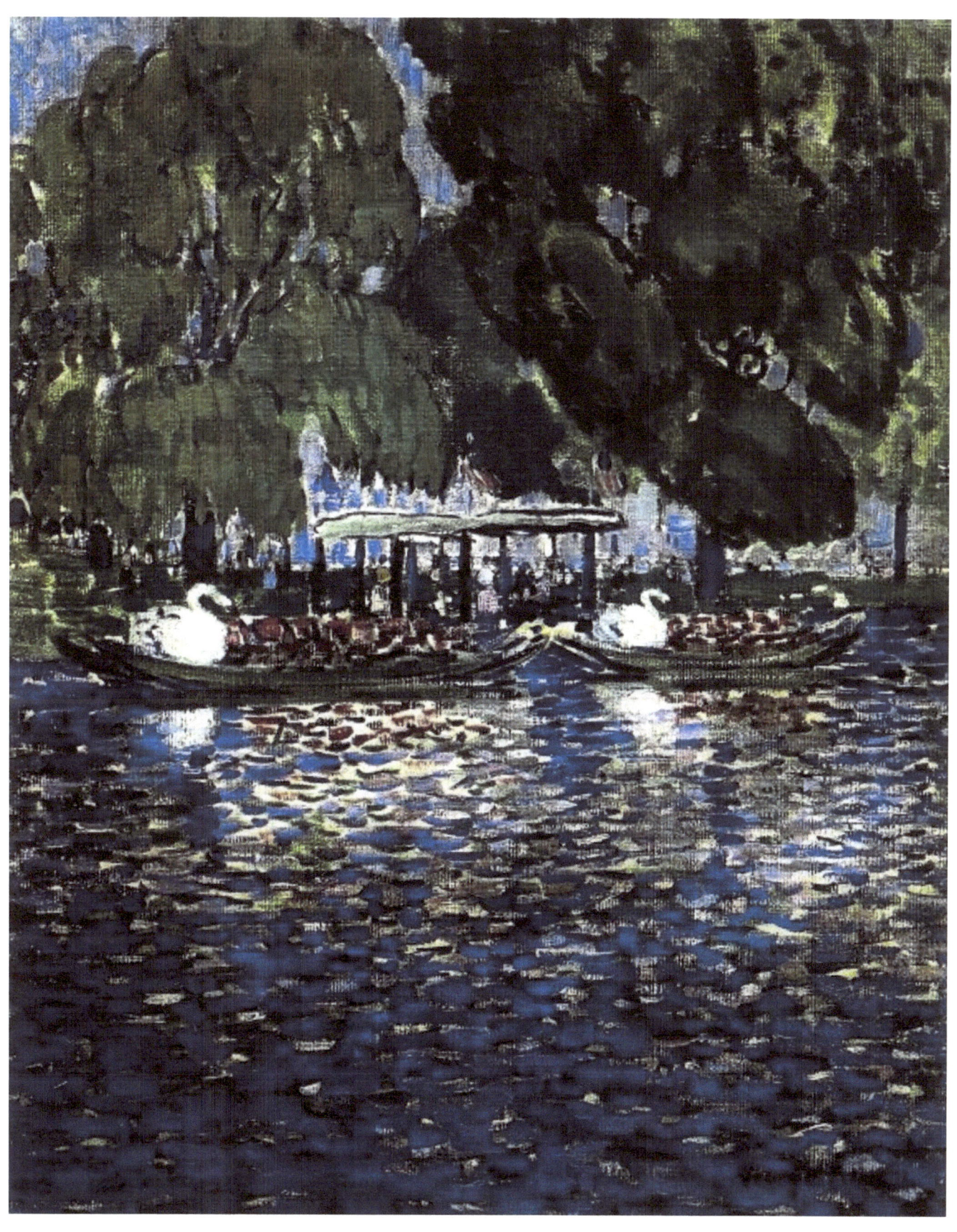

The Swan Boats, 1922
Oil on canvas

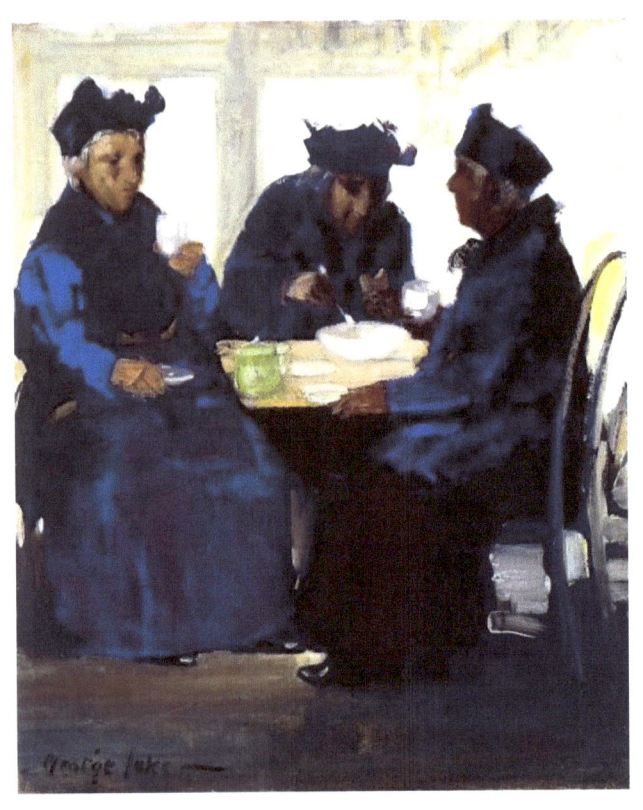

Tea Party, 1922
Oil on canvas

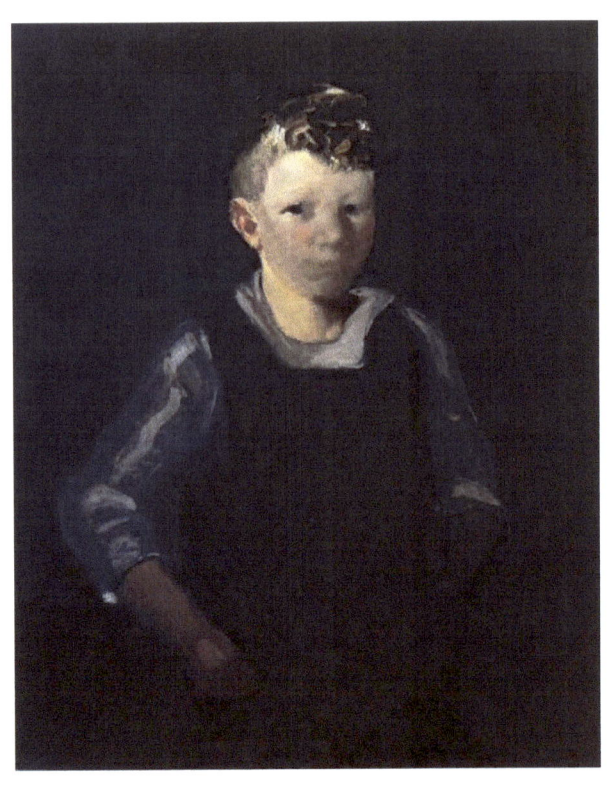

Patsy, the Cobbler
1923,Oil on canvas

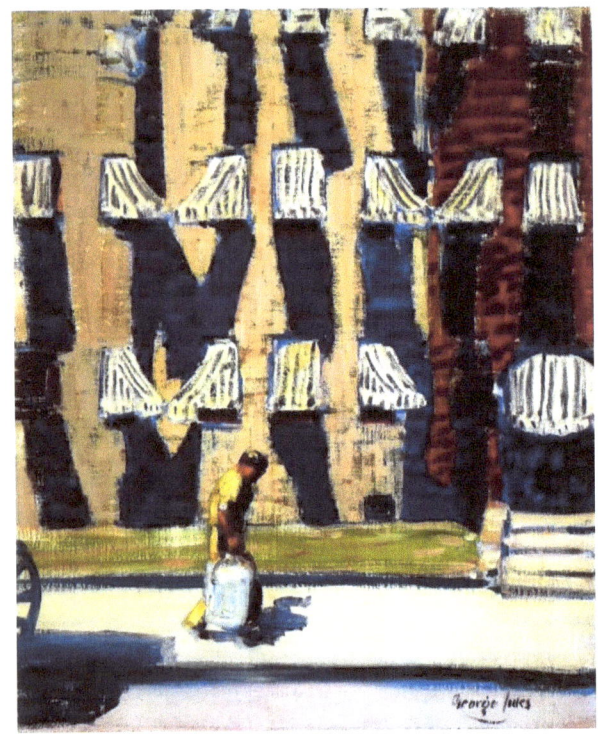

Noontime, St. Botolph Street, Boston, 1923
Oil on canvas

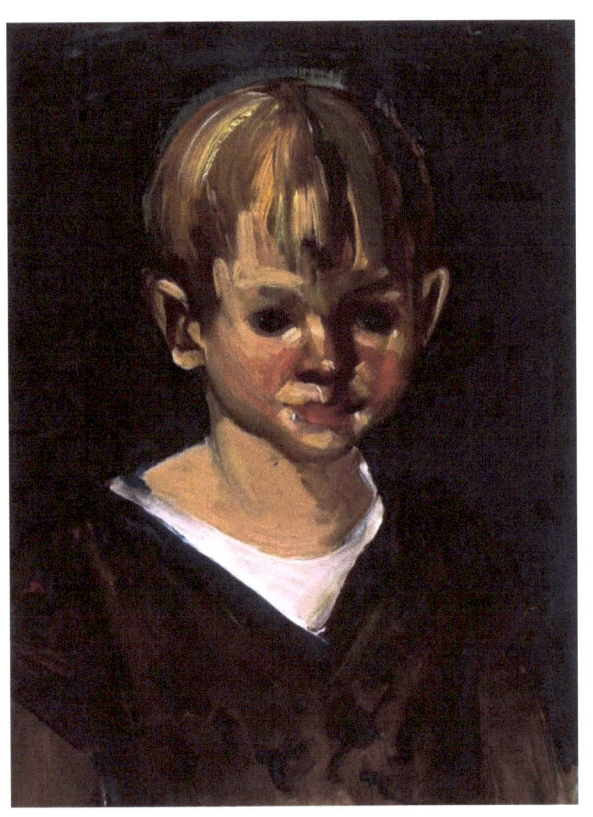

Young Boy, 1923
Oil on canvas

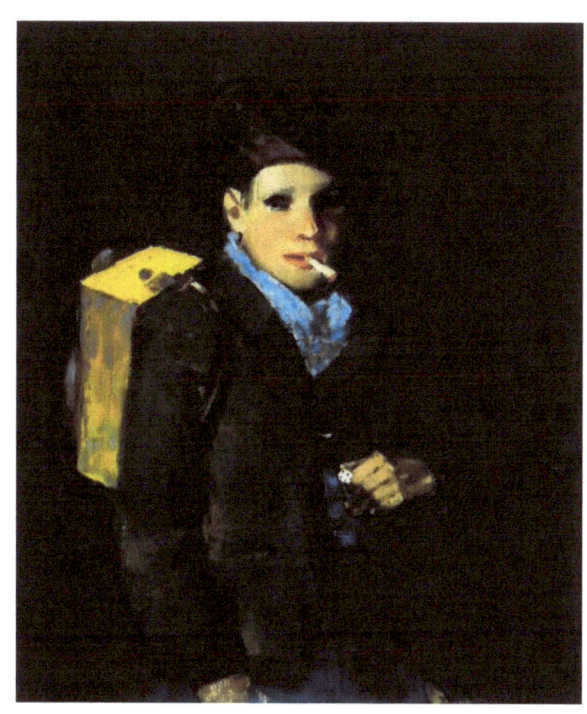

Boy with Dice 1924
Oil on canvas

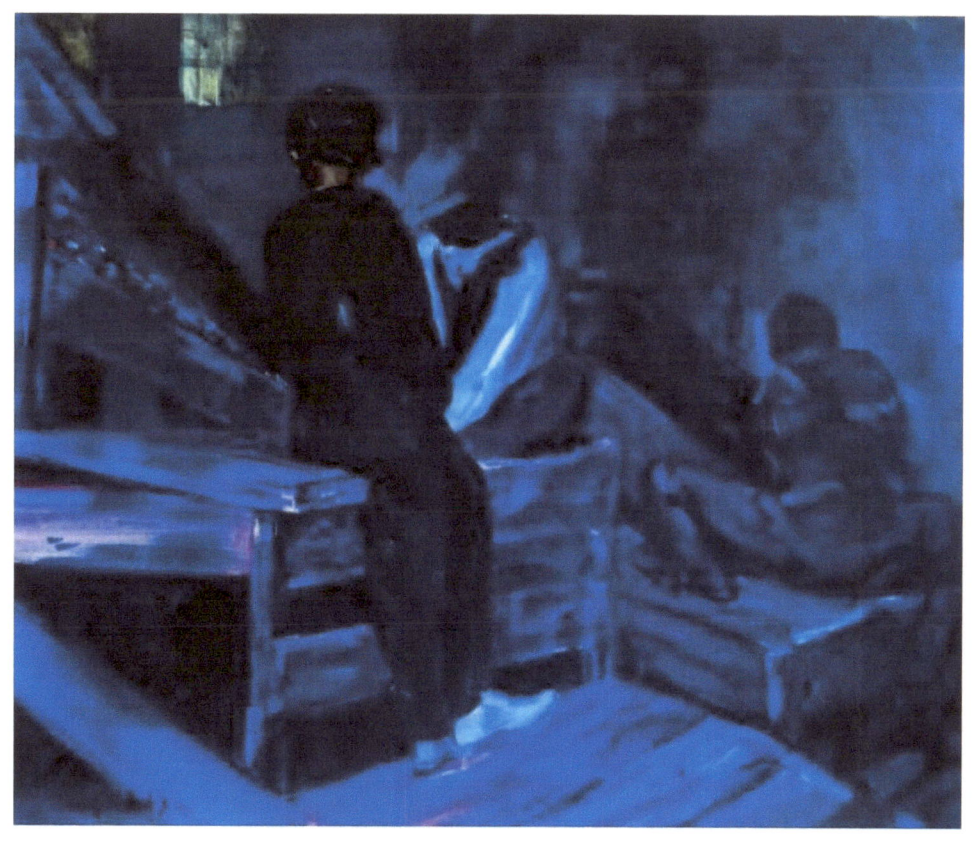

The Breaker Boys, 1925
Oil on canvas

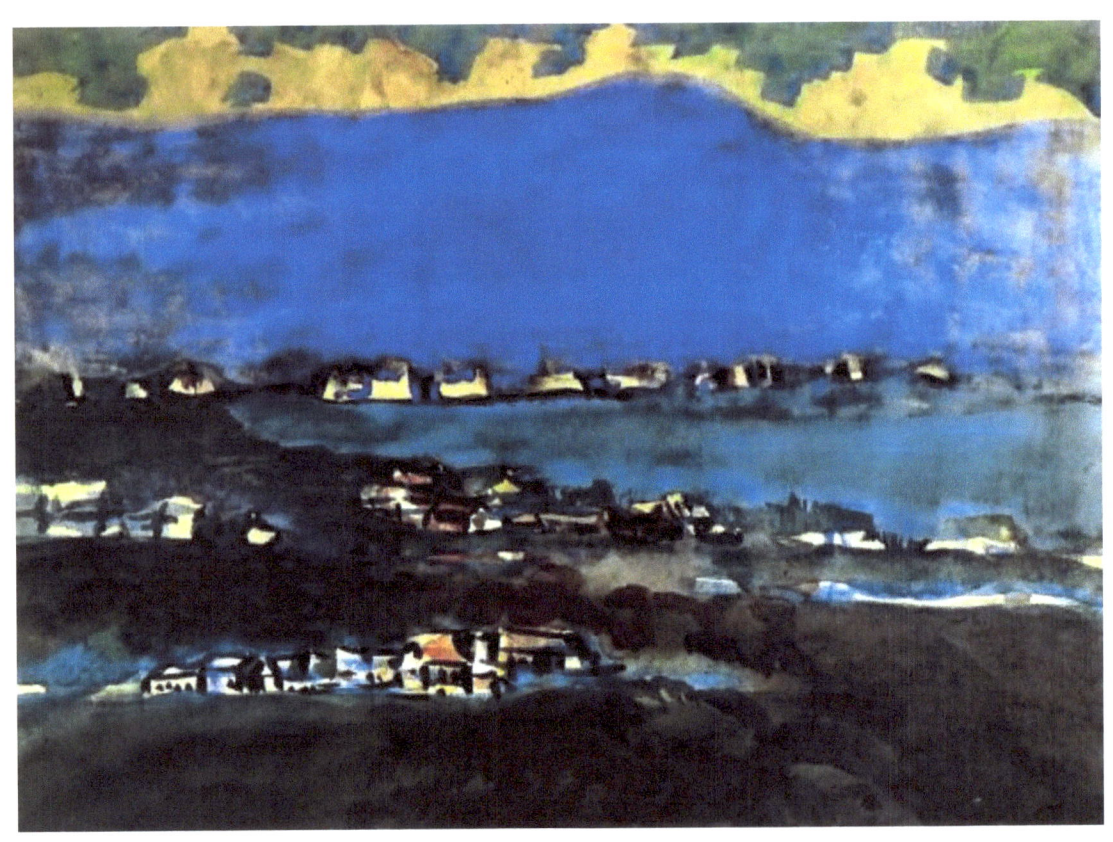

Coaltown, 1925, Oil on canvas

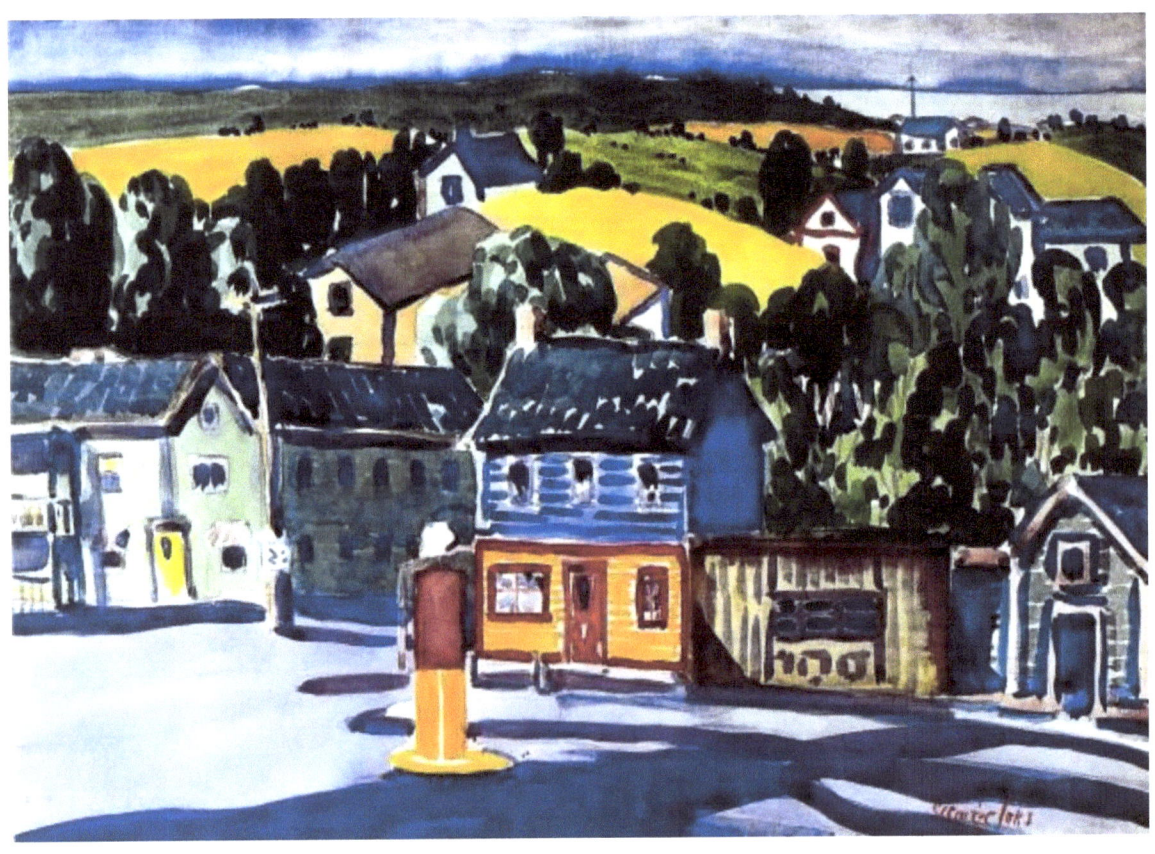

Gas Station, 1925, Oil on canvas

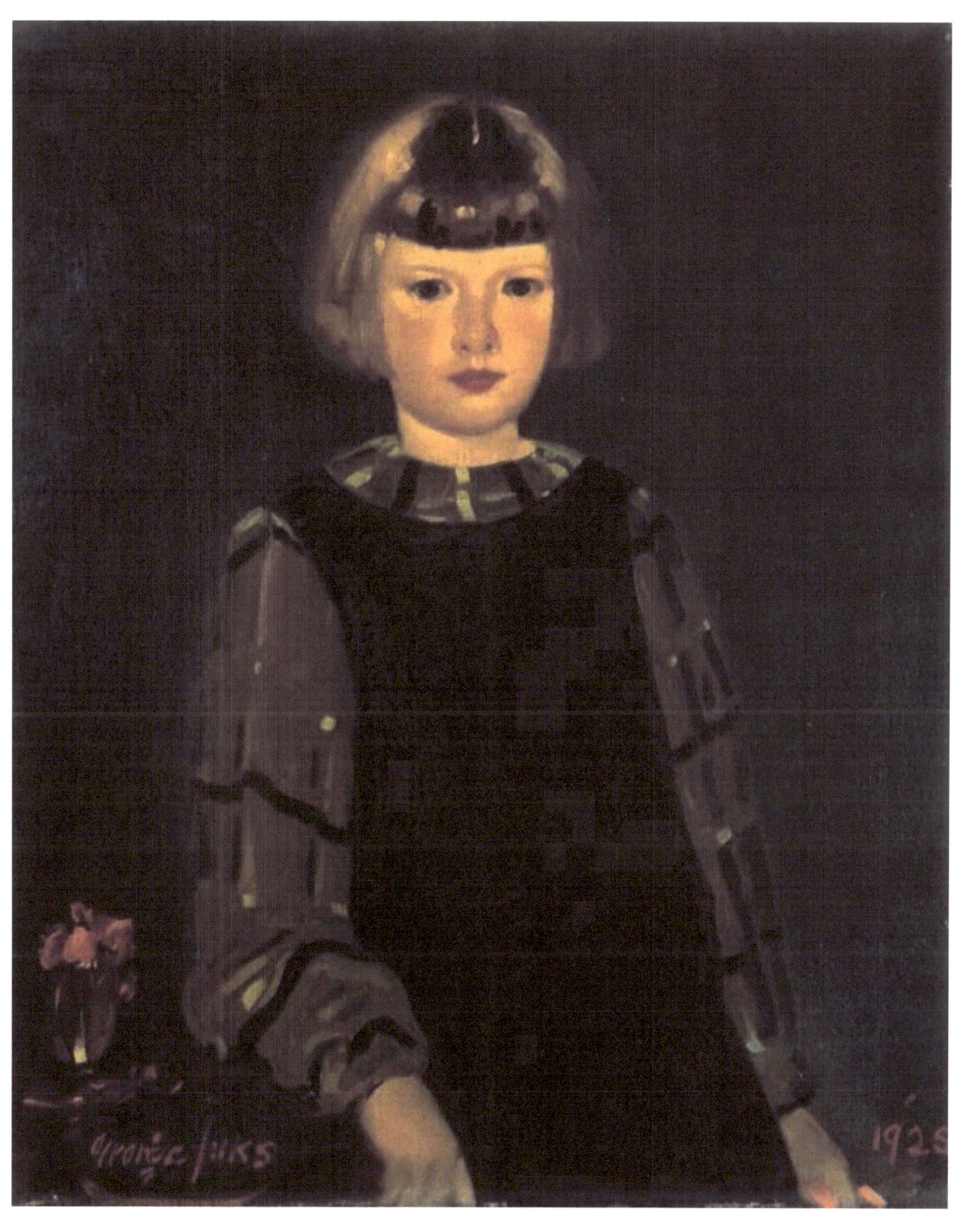

Girl, 1925
Oil on canvas

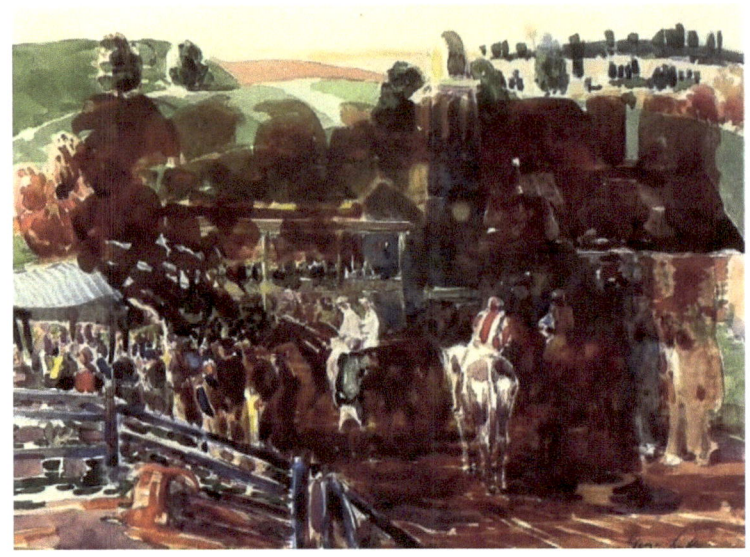

The Race Track, 1925
Oil on canvas

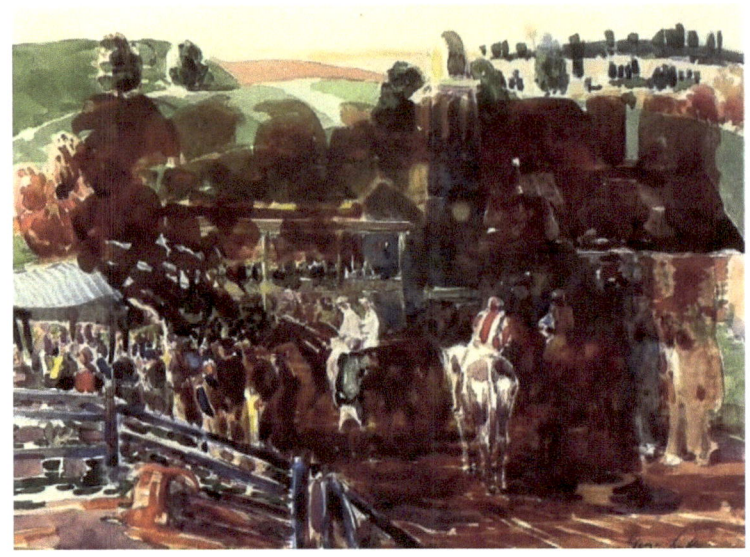

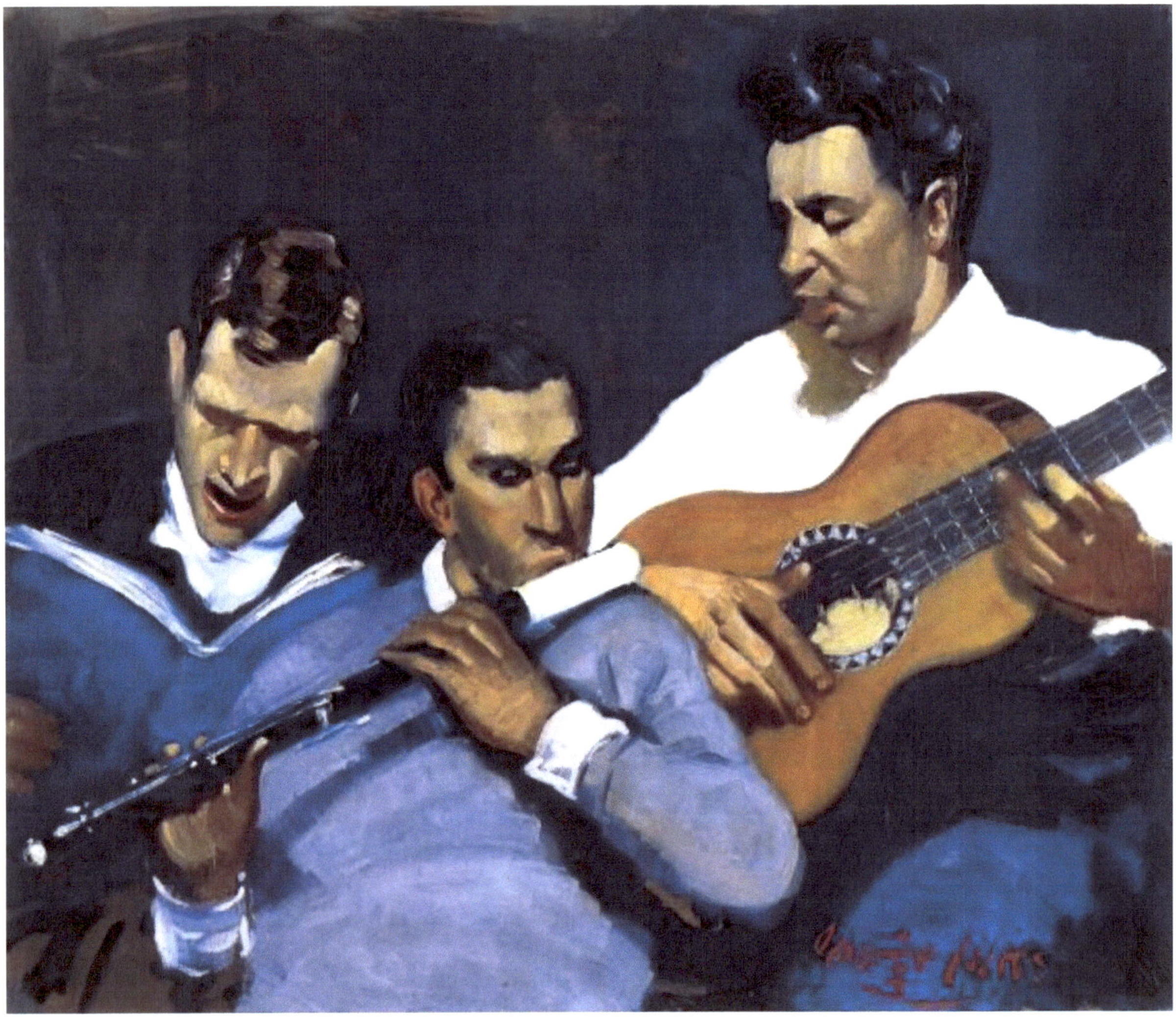

Three Top Sergeants, 1925

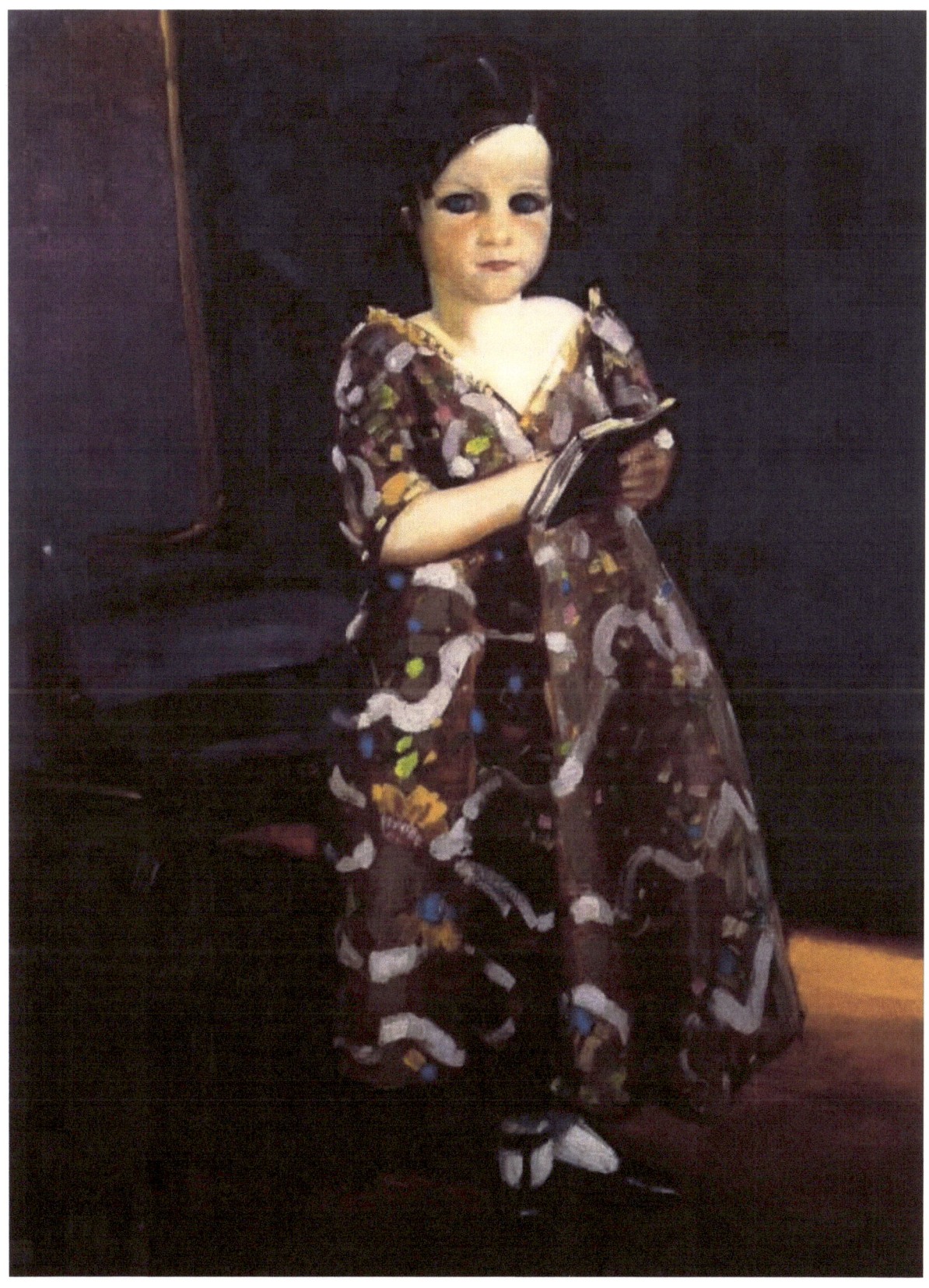

Jenny McKean as Infanta, 1926
Oil on canvas

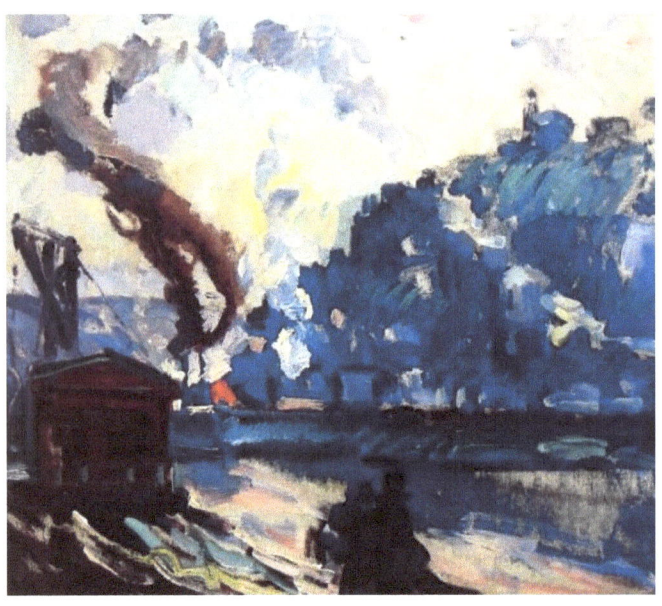

Morning Shadows, 1927
Oil on canvas

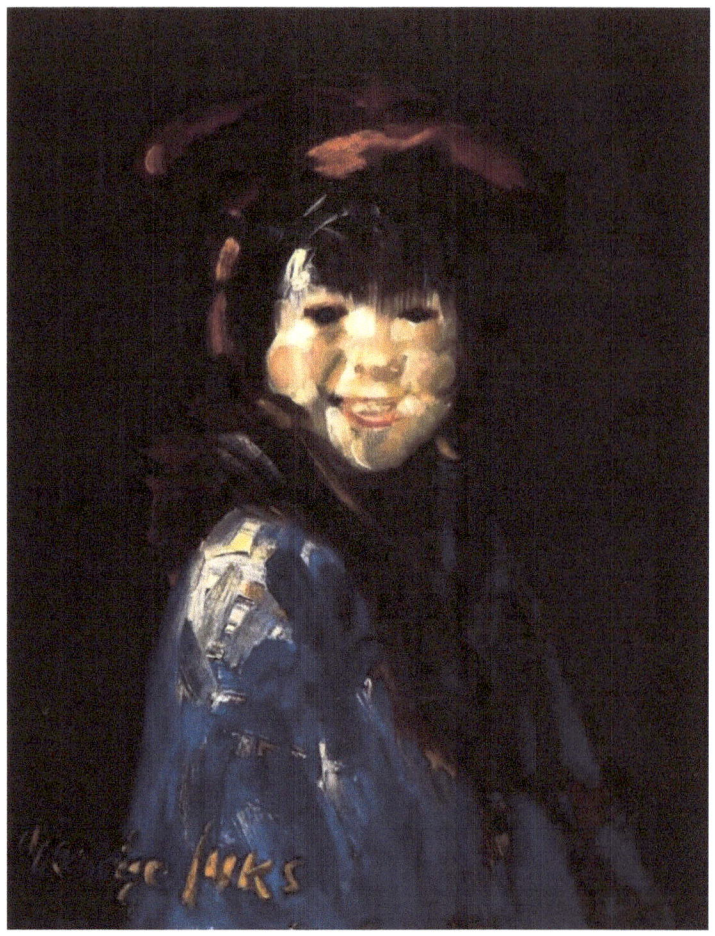

The Clown, 1928
Oil on canvas

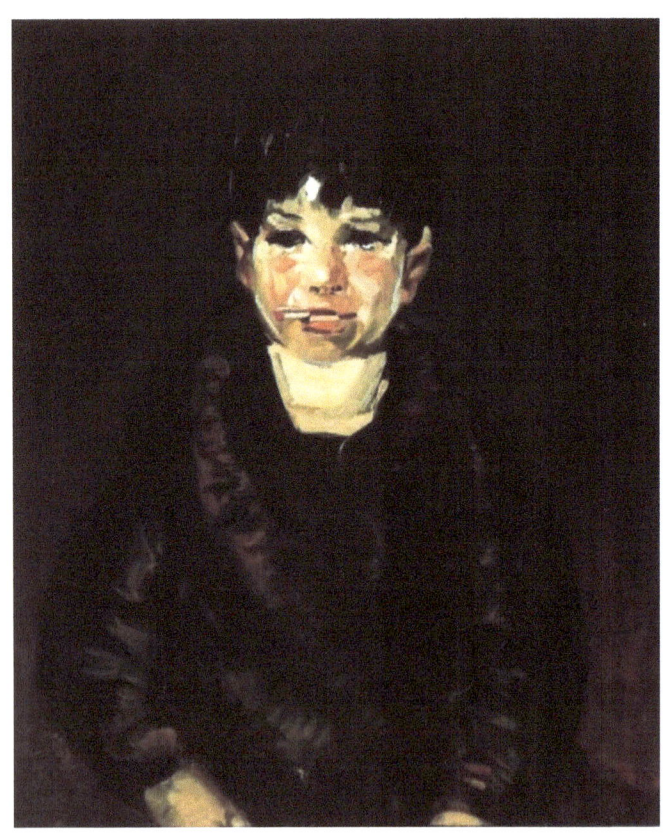

Butts, 1928
Oil on canvas

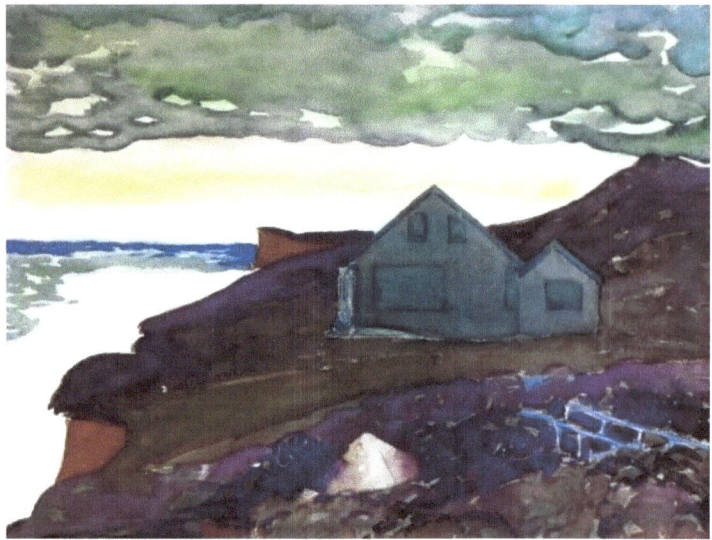

House on the Point, 1928, Oil on canvas

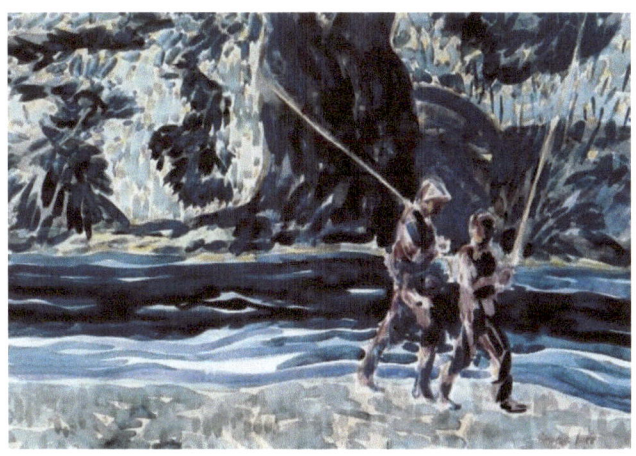

Trout Fishermen, Berk Hills 1928, Oil on
canvas

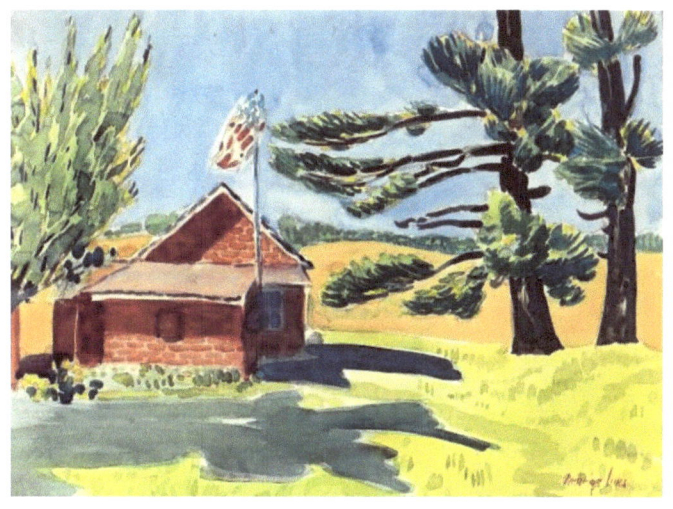

Old Schoolhouse, Ryders, 1929, Oil on
canvas

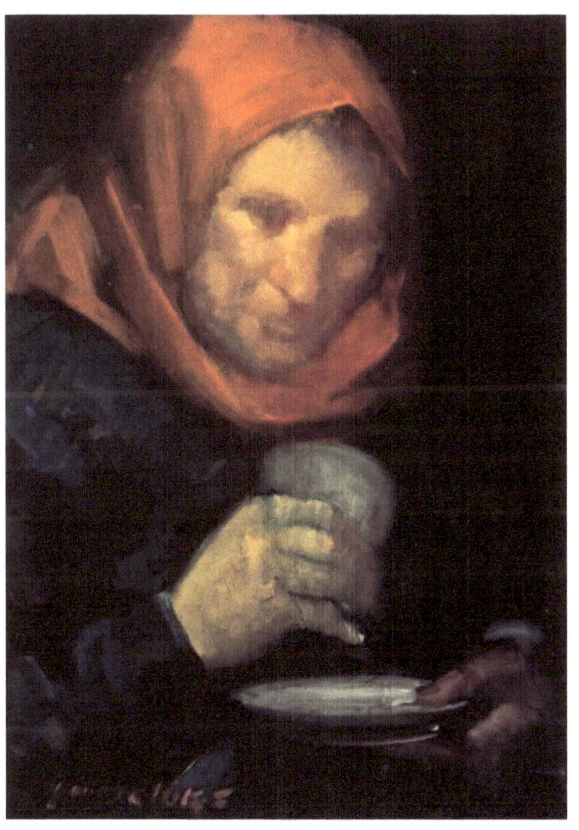

The Countess, 1929
Oil on canvas

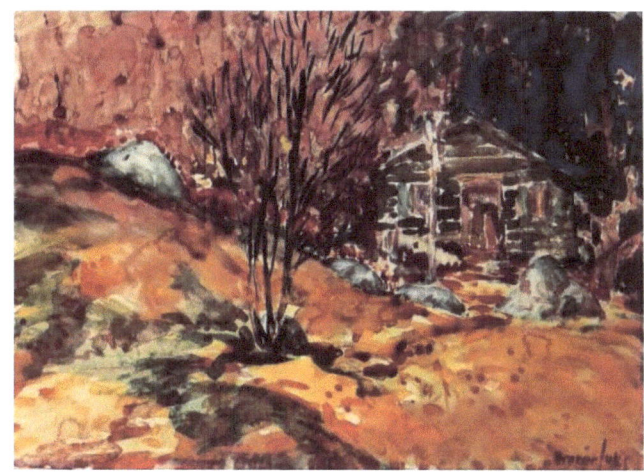

Autumn Landscape, 1930, Oil on canvas

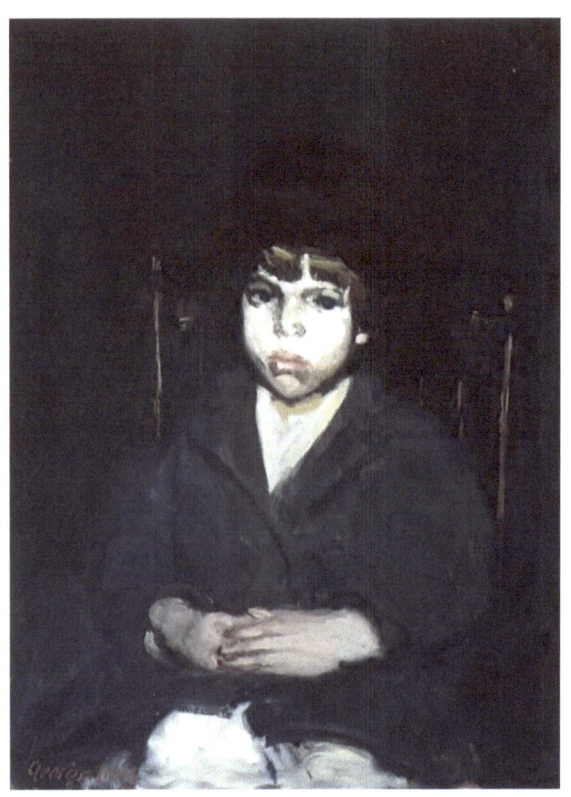

The Black Hat, Oil on canvas

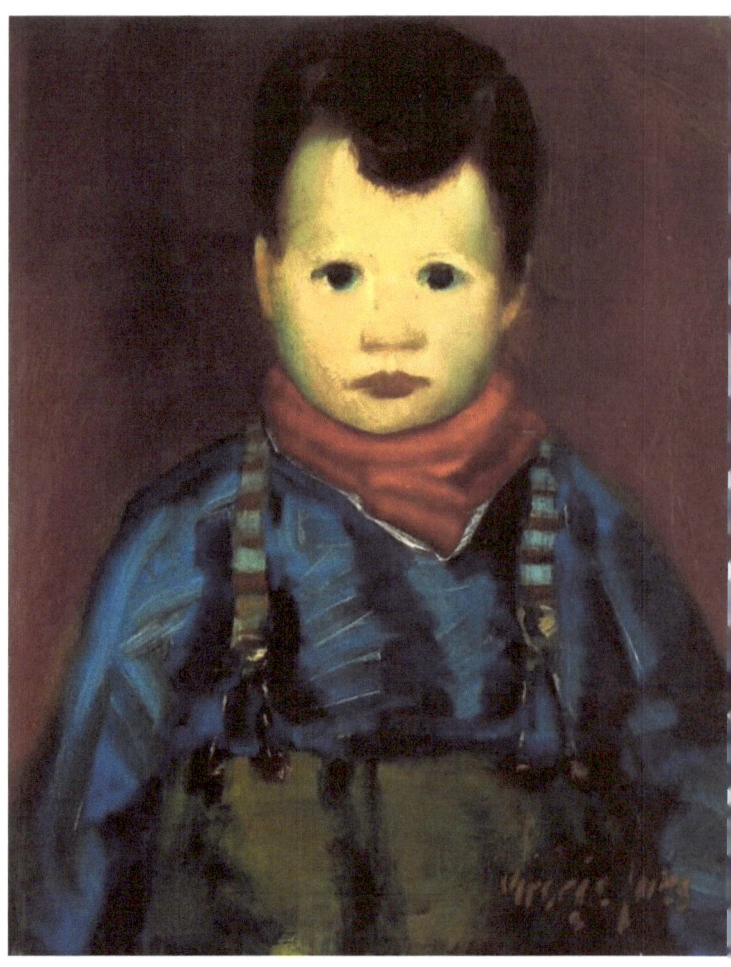

Boy with Suspenders
Oil on canvas

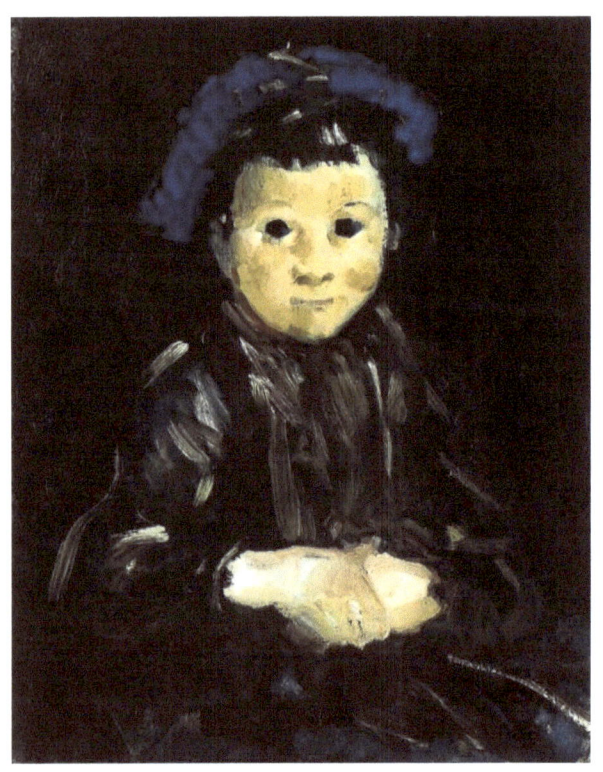

Boy with Blue Cap, Oil on canvas

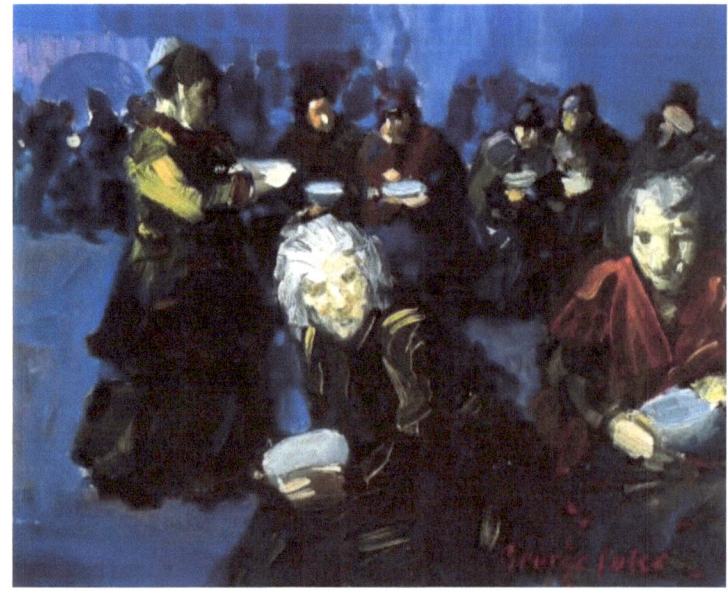

The Bread Line, Oil on canvas

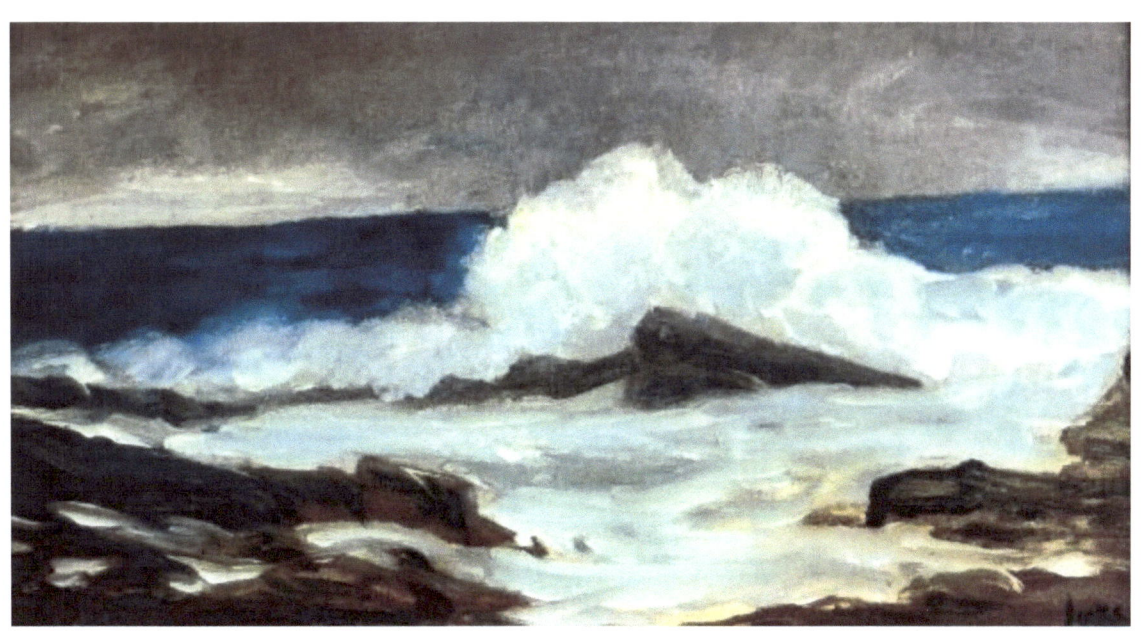

Breaking Surf
Oil on canvas

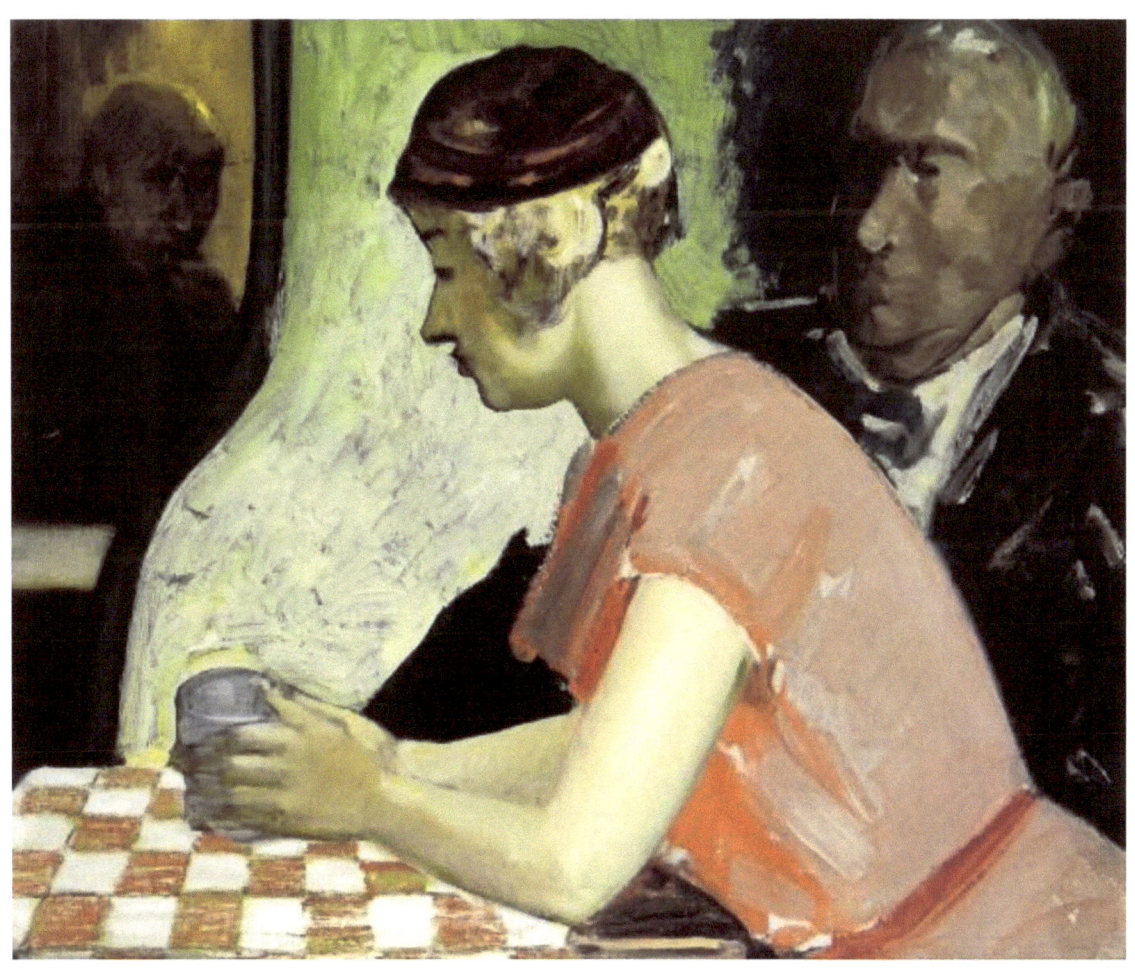

Cafe Scene - a Study of a Young Woman
Oil on canvas

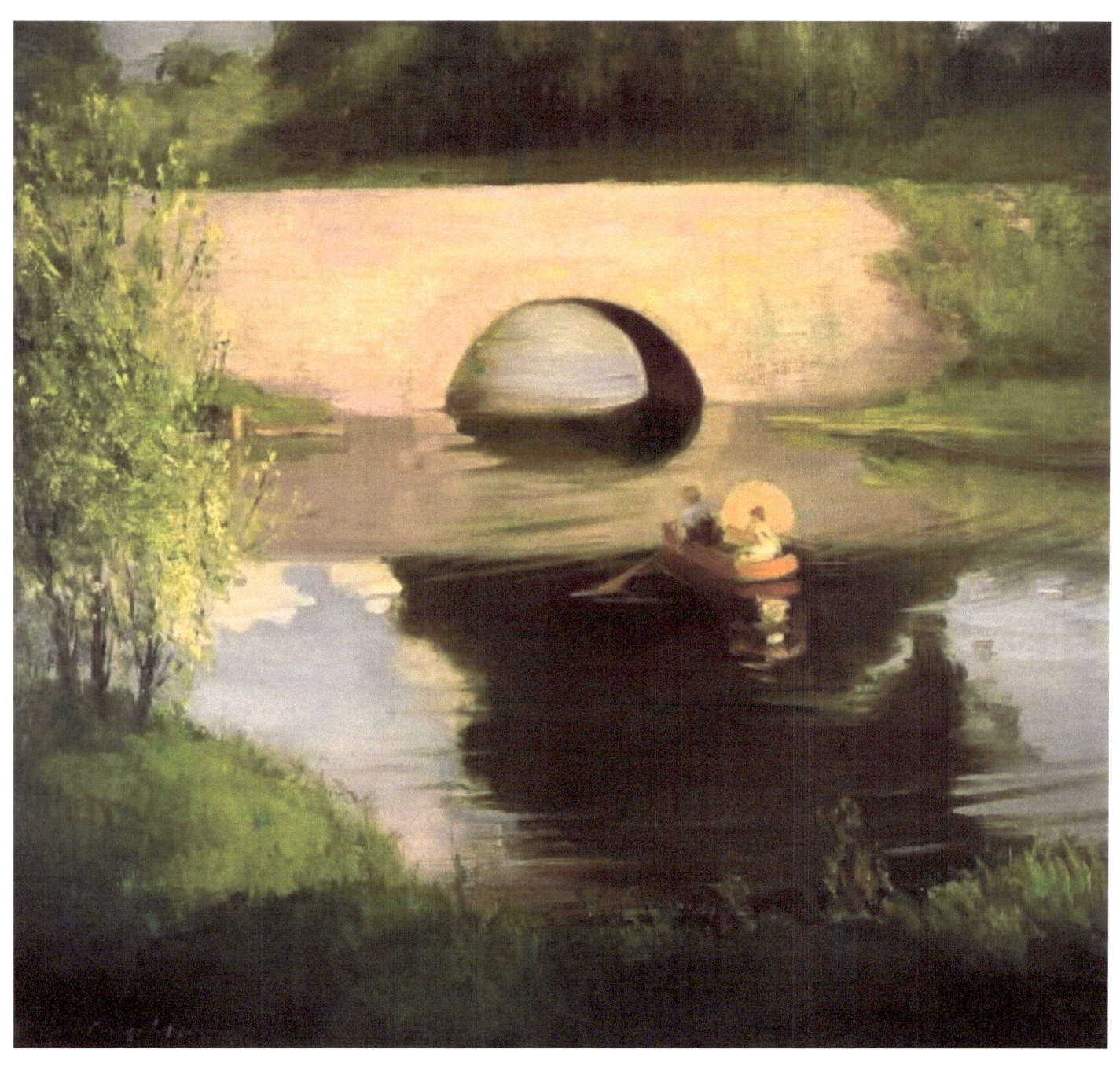

Central Park
Oil on canvas

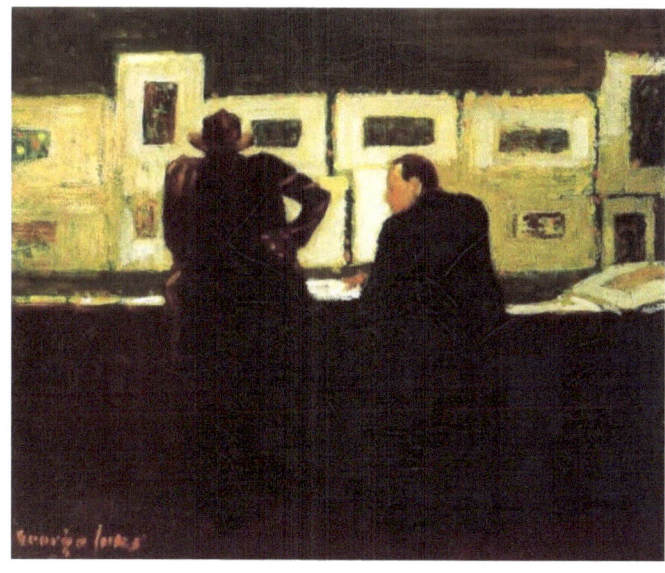

The Chapman Gallery
Oil on canvas

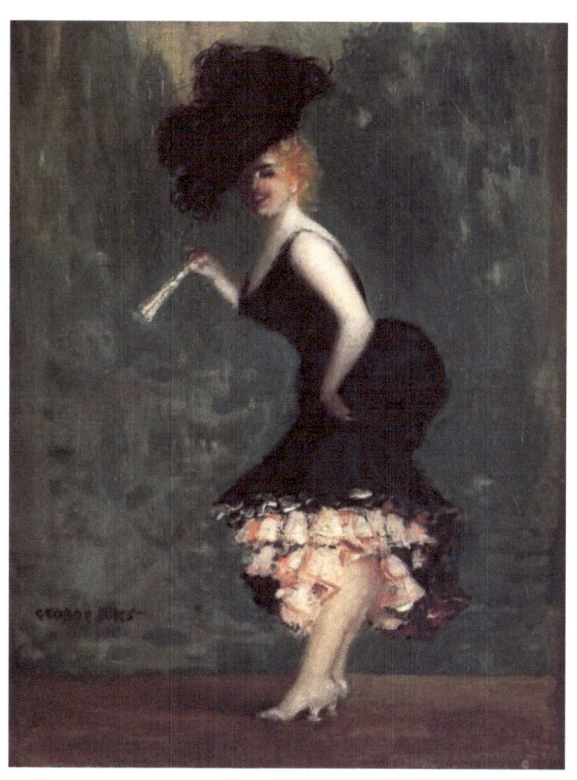

The Dancer
Oil on canvas

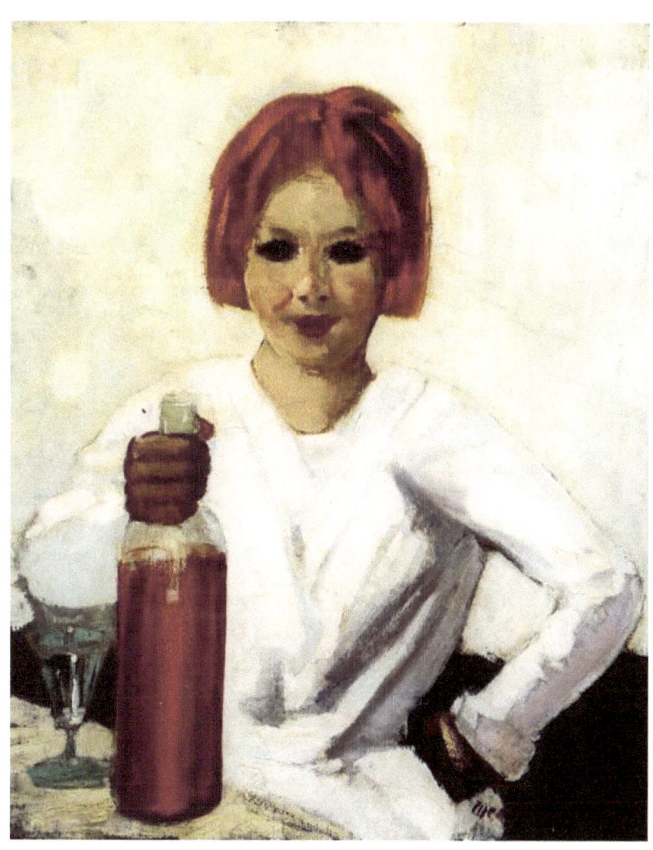

The Clown's Daughter
Oil on canvas

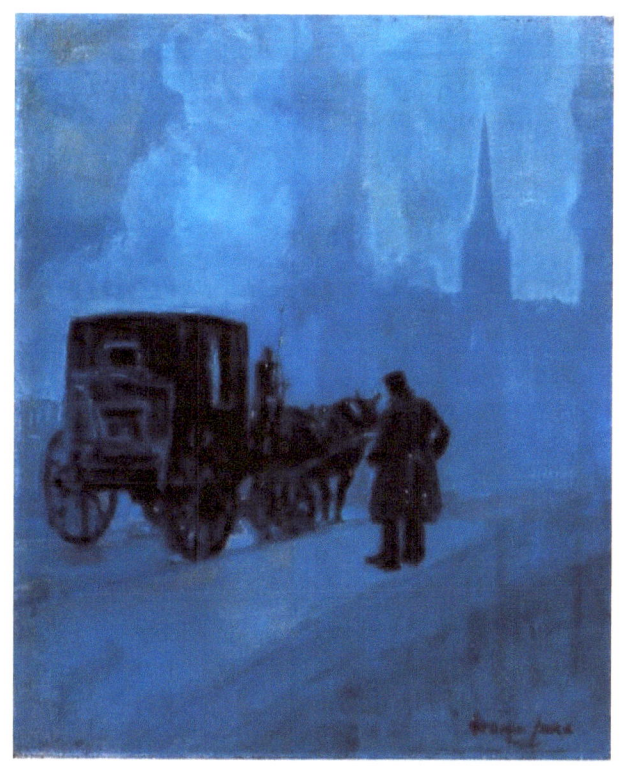

Foggy NIght, New York
Oil on canvas

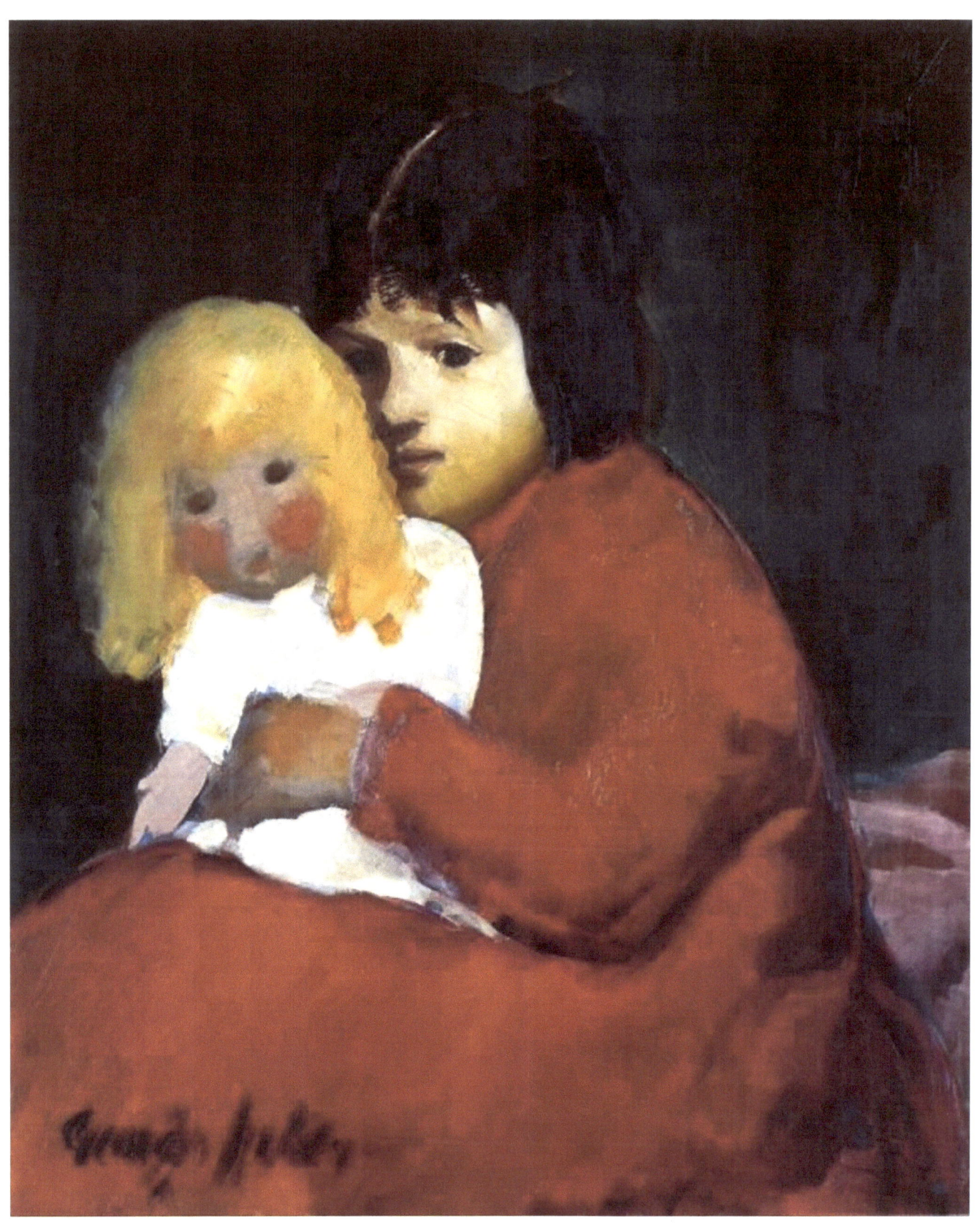

Girl with Doll
Oil on canvas

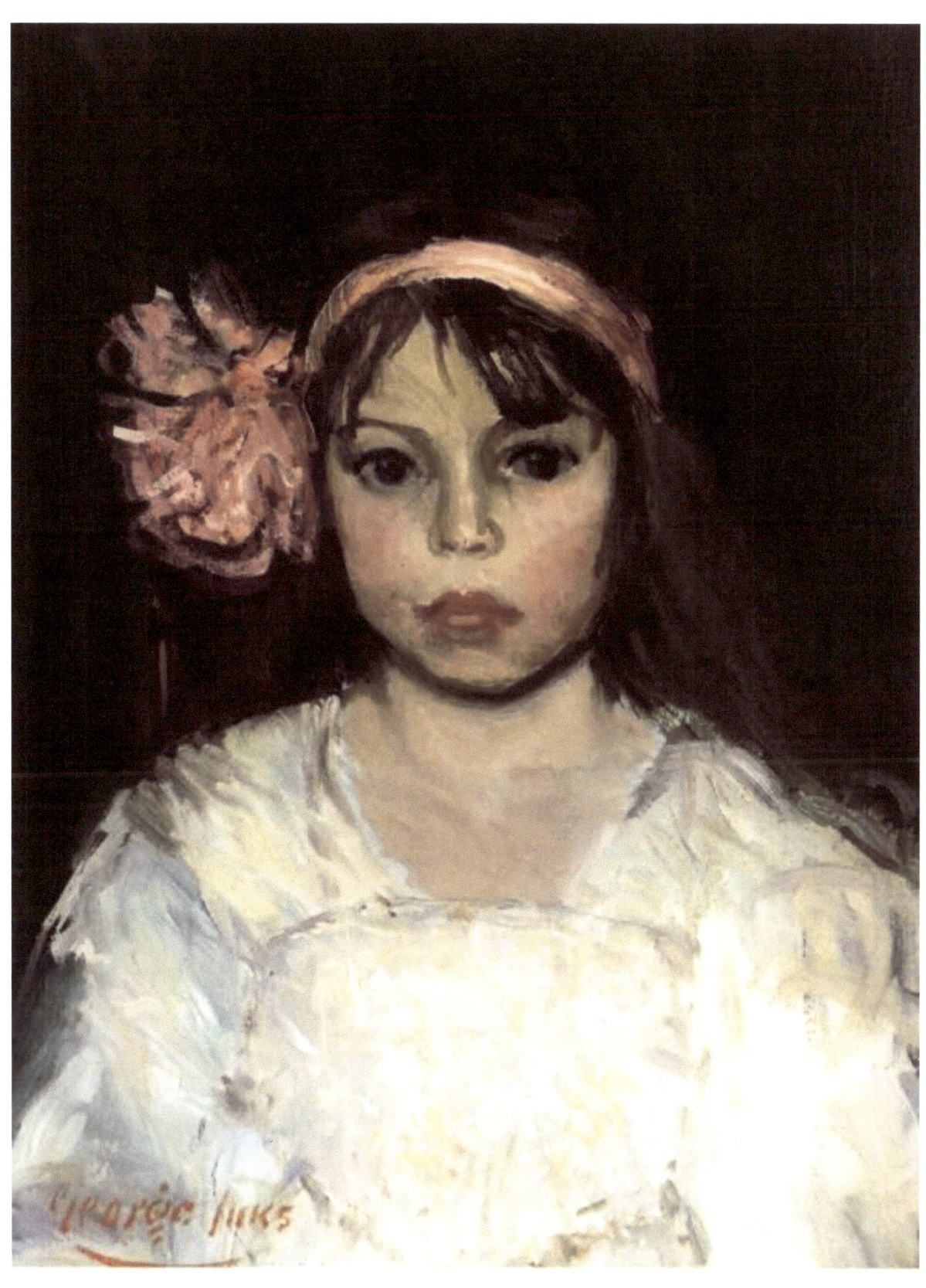

Girl with Pink Ribbon
Oil on canvas

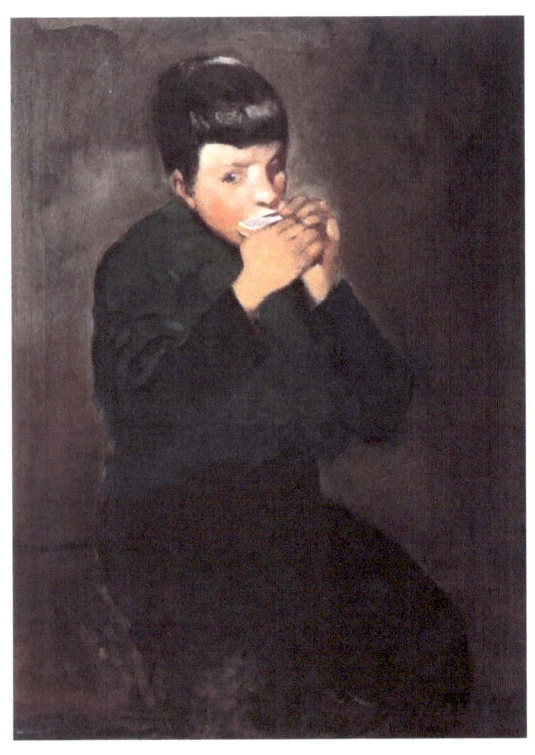

The Harmonica Player
Oil on canvas

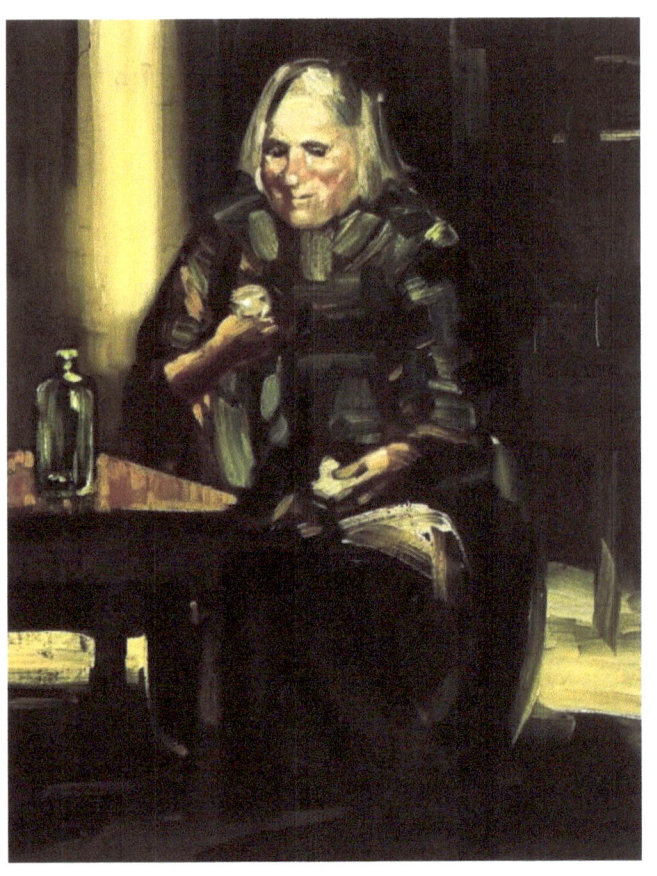

The Hole in the Wall
Oil on canvas

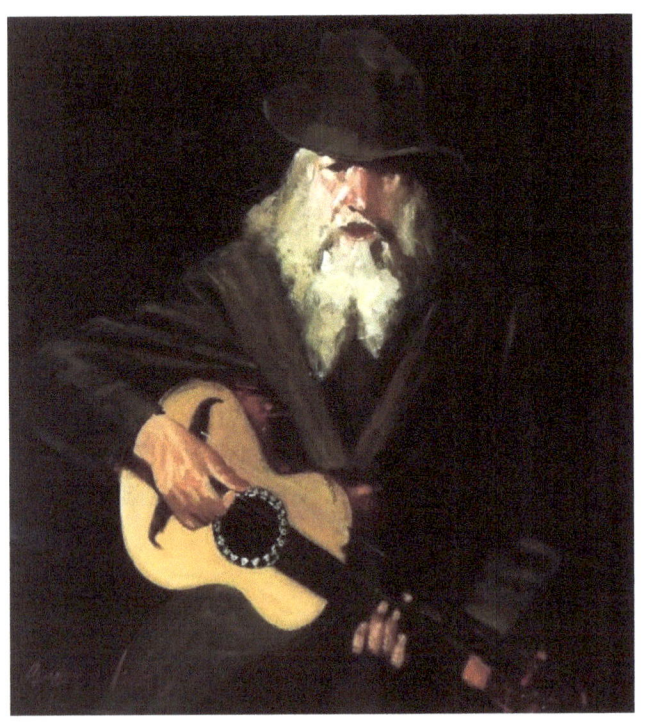

Hobo Musician
Oil on canvas

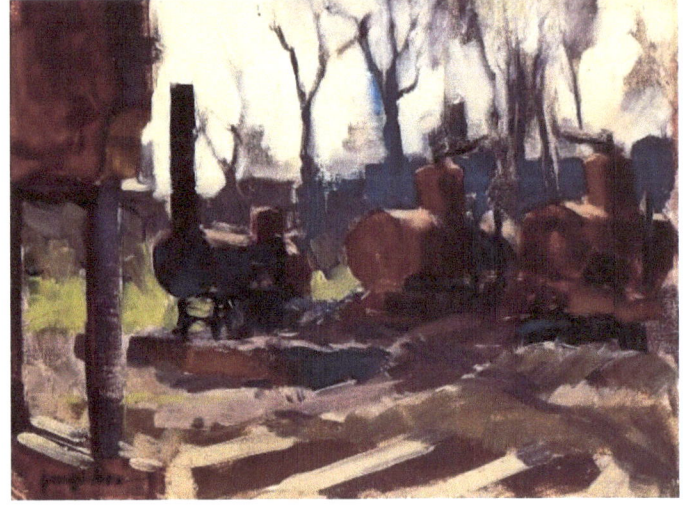

Industrial Landscape, Oil on canvas

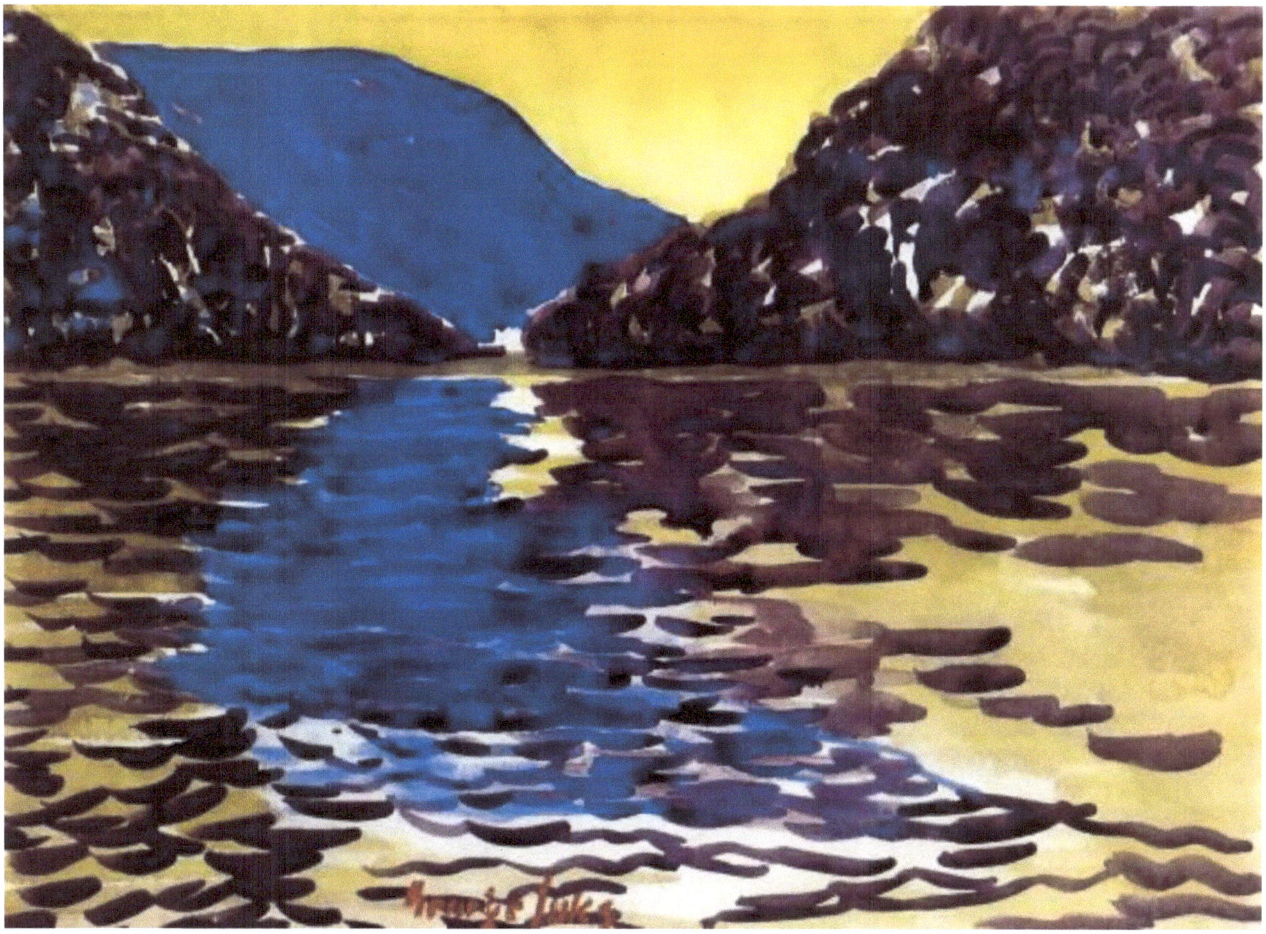

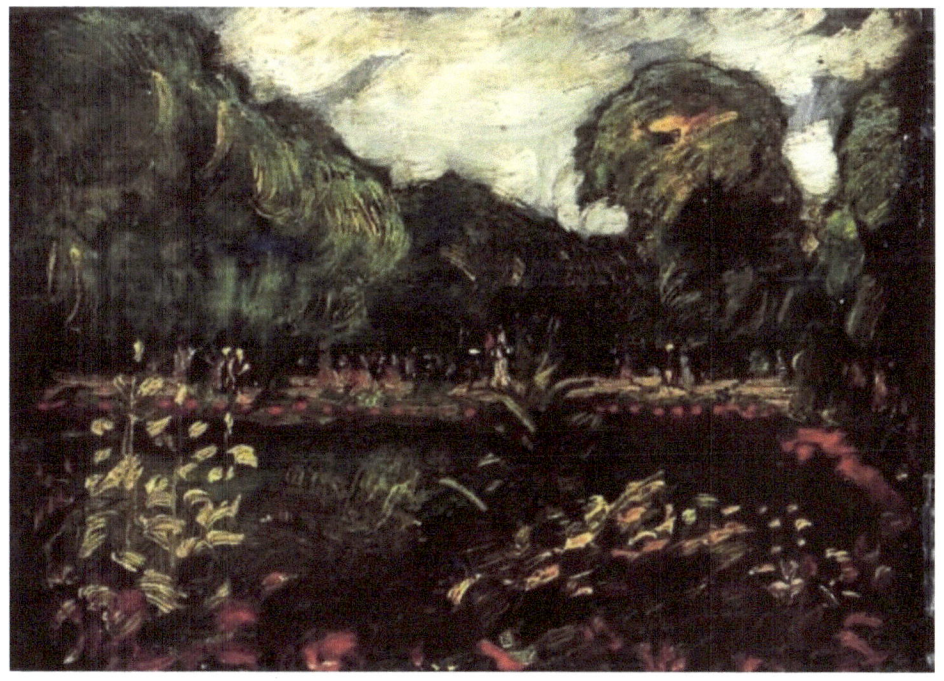

Lower Ausable Lake, Adirondacks, Oil on canvas

Main Entrance, Luxembourg Garden, Paris
Oil on canvas

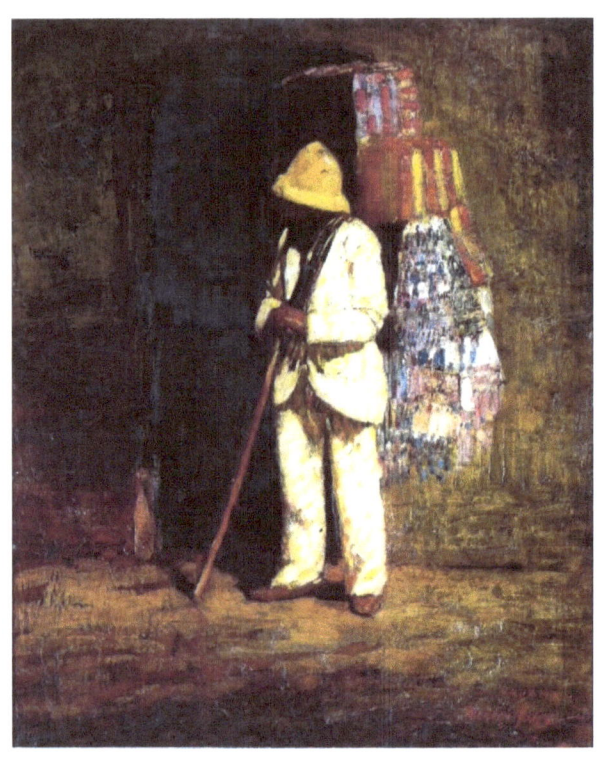

Man in Havana
Oil on canvas

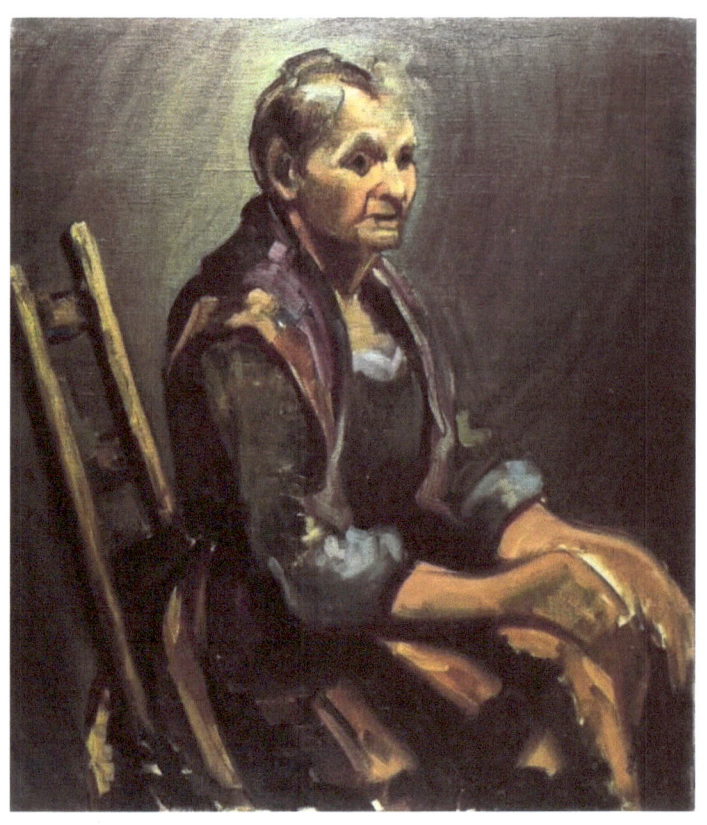

Old Woman
Oil on canvas

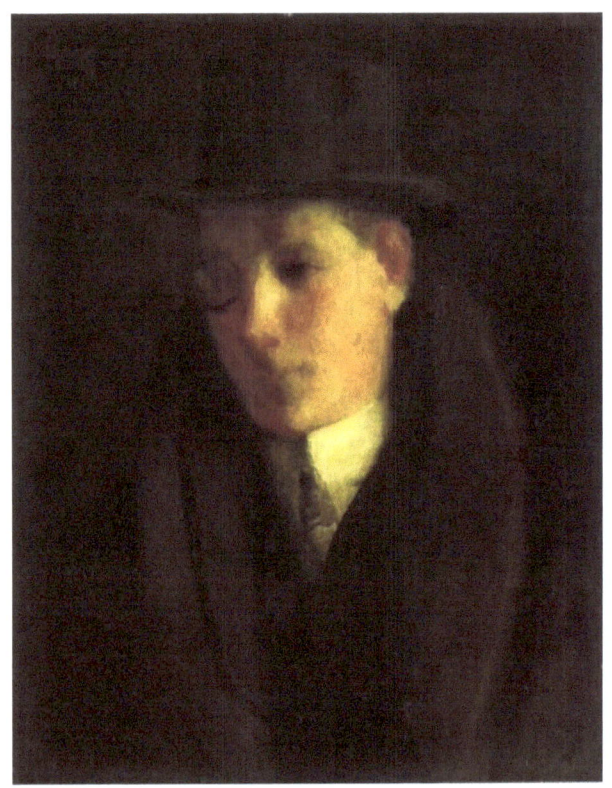

Man with a Monocle
Oil on canvas

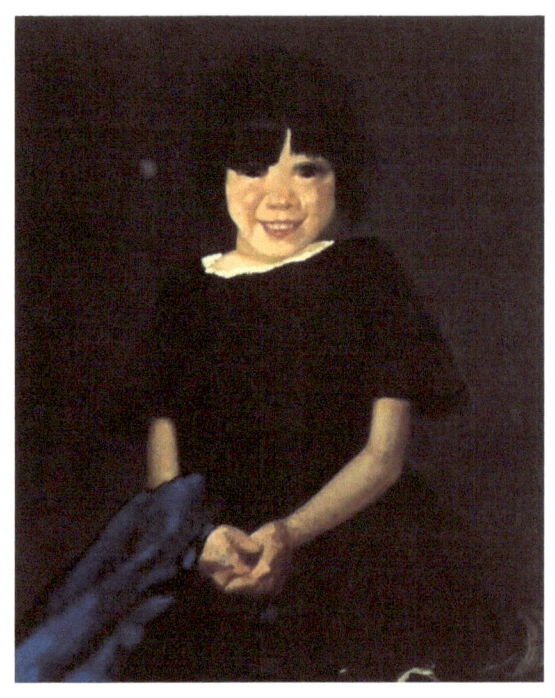

Portrait of a Girl in Black
Oil on canvas

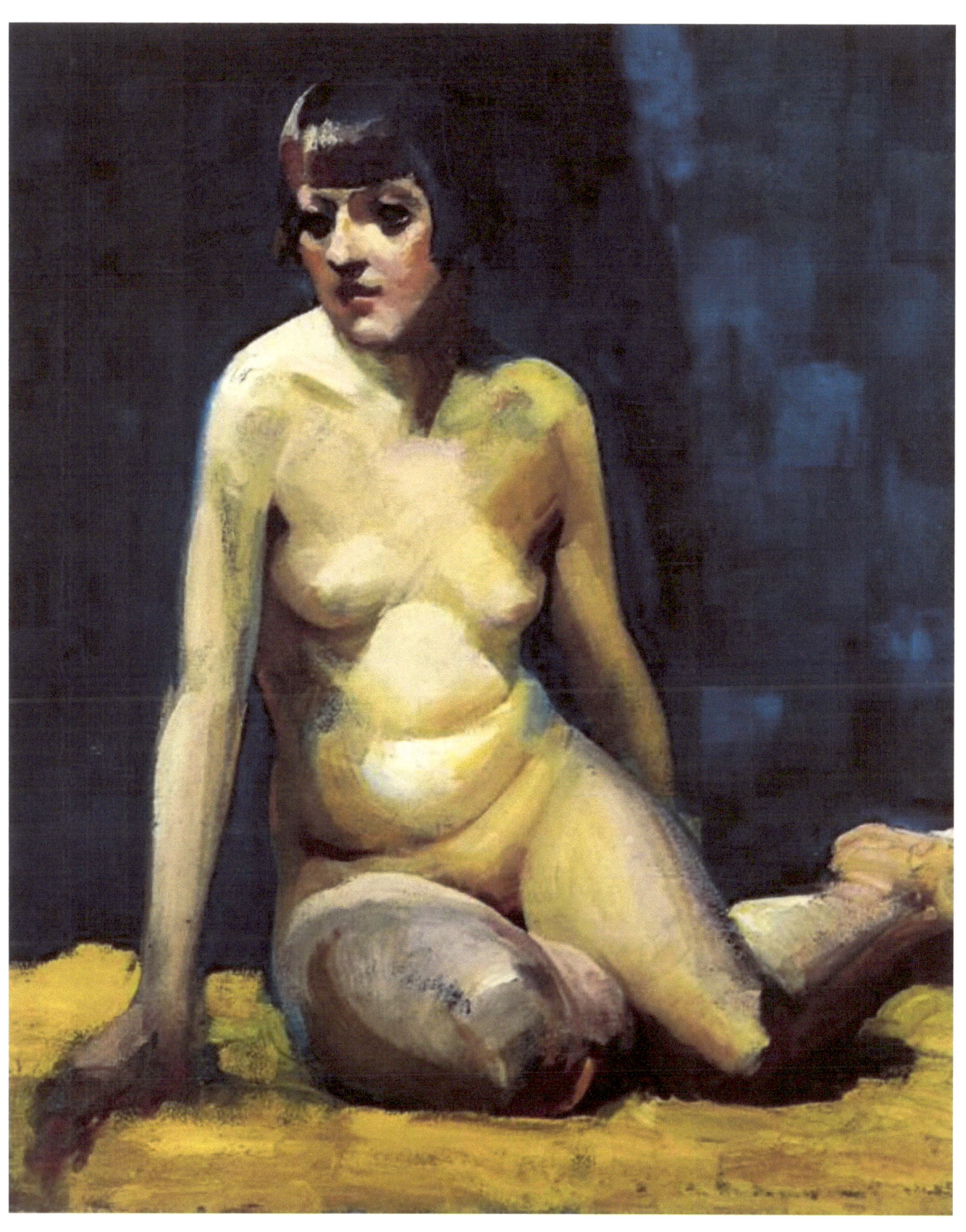

Seated Nude with Bobbed Hair
Oil on canvas

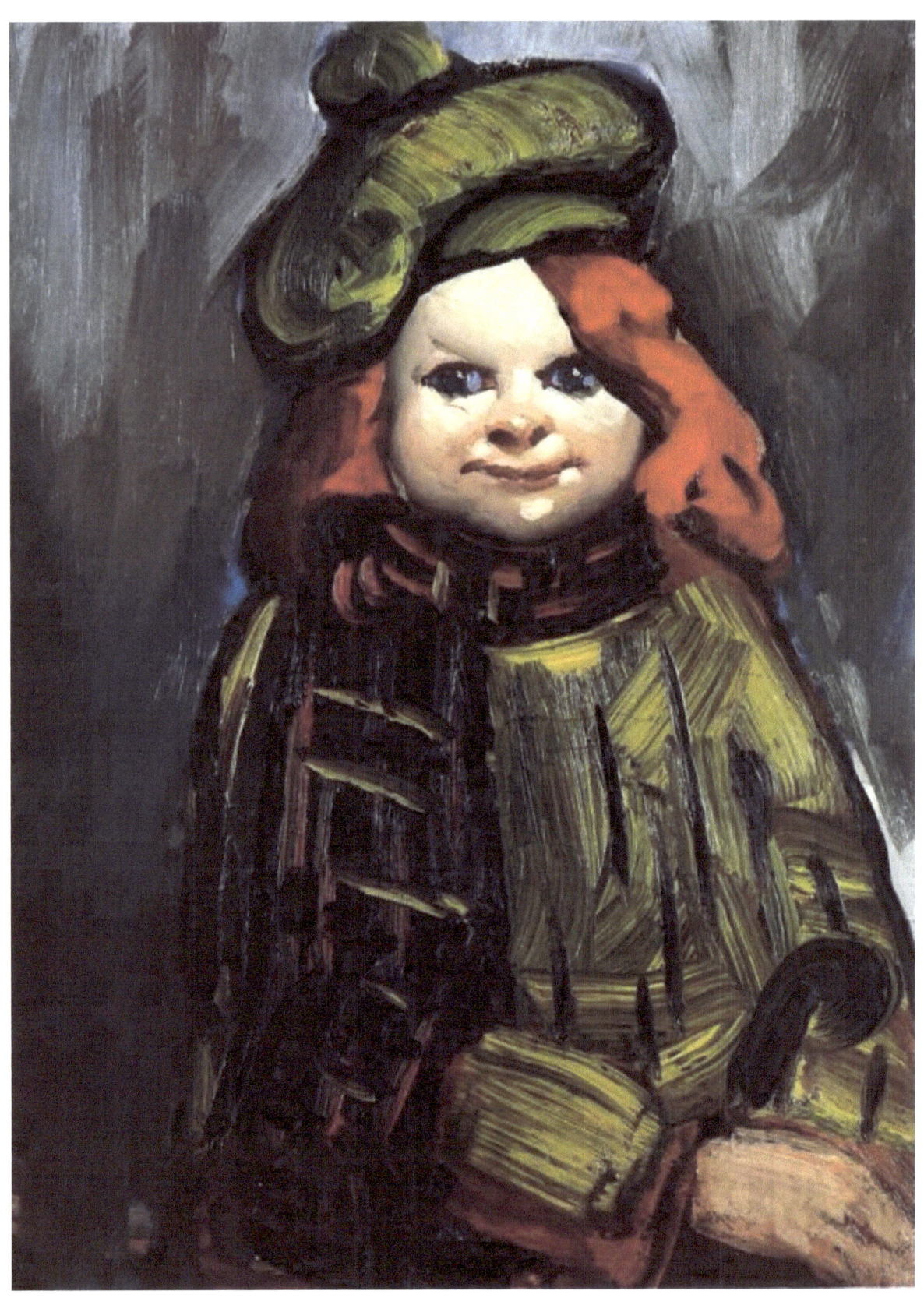

Tom
Oil on canvas

www.ingramcontent.com/pod-product-compliance
Lightning Source LLC
Chambersburg PA
CBHW050838180526

45159CB00004B/1946